Child Development

An illustrated guide

Carolyn Meggitt and Gerald Sunderland

Heinemann Educational Publishers,
Halley Court, Jordan Hill, Oxford OX2 8EJ
A division of Reed Educational & Professional Publishing Ltd

Heinemann is a registered trademark of Reed Educational & Professional Publishing Limited

OXFORD MELBOURNE AUCKLAND JOHANNESBURG BLANTYRE GABORONE IBADAN
PORTSMOUTH NH (USA) CHICAGO

First published 2000
2004 2003 2002 2001
10 9 8 7 6 5 4 3

A catalogue record for this book is available from the British Library on request.

ISBN 0 435 42056 9

All photographs including the cover design and photograph by Gerald Sunderland.

Pages designed and typeset by Brian Melville @ big red hat.

Printed and bound in Spain by Edelvives.

Tel.: 01865 888058 www.heinemann.co.uk

Acknowledgements

We would like to thank the following people for their valuable assistance in producing this book: the parents of all the babies and children whose photographs appear in the book; the children for their patience and co-operation; Dana Hepburn for resourcing many of the children for the photographs in Sections One and Two; Brenda Tebby, Professional Development Manager, Queen Mary's Maternity Unit at West Middlesex University Hospital, for her patient assistance in taking the photographs of newborn babies; Susan Burch, Special Needs Department, The Cornwallis School; Sarah Fletcher, Team Leader, Pauline Johnson, Physiotherapist, and all the staff at Maidstone Children's Centre, for their guidance and help in taking the photographs for the section on children with special needs; Cate Sunderland, Headteacher, Oaklands School, for resourcing the children for the photograph on the back cover; Mrs James, Headteacher, St James's RC Primary School, for resourcing some of the children for Section One; Claire McCann, Headteacher, Carlisle Infant School, for resourcing some of the children for Section Two, Chapter 15. Thanks also to TP Activity Toys for the loan of the climbing frame for the cover photograph.

Thanks also to: Mary James, Publisher, for her enthusiasm and professional guidance; Sarah Garbett and Brian Melville for their design; and Andrew Nash for his expertise in editing the text.

Contents

Foreword

It is a great pleasure to write a foreword for this book. It states that it is a 'source of guidance for you in providing for the child's developmental needs': I am sure that it will.

This book takes account of two important aspects of the study of child development. Firstly, it describes the biological sequences of development, in ways which are easy to follow and learn.

Secondly, it updates the traditional approach to the study of child development pioneered by outstanding people in the field, such as Mary Sheridan. This is because, alongside the biological aspects, it also places emphasis on the socio-cultural part of the way children develop.

This will be one of those books which you will want to keep near you, to dip into as a useful resource, which you will revisit again and again ...

Tina Bruce
Honorary Visiting Professor
Faculty of Humanities and Education (Early Childhood Education)
University of North London

Introduction

The idea for this book was conceived in response to the growth of child-care courses worldwide. Many books focus on child development, but no other educational book offers a concise pictorial guide to the general development of children from birth right through to the age of 8 years.

Children across the world seem to pass through the same sequences of development, and within the same broad timetables. Although the pattern is broadly the same for all children, it is important to remember that each child is unique. Nevertheless, understanding the typical pattern will help you to develop your skills both in promoting children's health and in stimulating their all-round (or holistic) development.

The different areas of development are inter-related. The ideas, language, communication, feelings, relationships and other cultural elements among which each child is brought up influence his or her development profoundly.

Children with special needs often seem to dance the developmental ladder – they move through developmental stages in unusual and very uneven ways. For example, they might sit or walk at the usual age, but not talk at the usual age.

Mary Sheridan's valuable research in the 1950s provides a useful framework for the study of child development. This book extends Sheridan's work by incorporating additional research from many other experts in the field.

Simply reading statements about what a child at a given age is expected to achieve can prove very dull. We believe that presenting this information alongside photographs of real children will bring the subject of child development alive.

Using this book

Using this book has many benefits
Firstly, the book provides reassurance when a child is developing normally. Equally, it enables you to identify those children who for some reason may not be following normative stages. Secondly, the descriptions given will help you build up a picture of a child's progress over a period of time. Thirdly, they will also enable you to anticipate, and to respond appropriately to, certain types of age-related behaviour – for example,

separation anxiety. Finally, and perhaps most importantly of all, the book is an invaluable source of guidance for you in providing for the child's developmental needs.

Qualifications in child care and education

The book focuses on the areas of development defined by the leading organisations in the UK that award qualifications in child care and education, namely CACHE (Council for Awards in Children's Care and Education), City & Guilds and EDEXCEL/BTEC. Remember that the stages or 'milestones' of development described are *normative* indicators of development – they can only indicate general trends in development in children across the world.

Every child is unique

There are, inevitably, some drawbacks in using normative descriptions. For example, they may cause unnecessary anxiety when a child does not achieve 'milestones' that are considered normal for a given age. Remember that the individual child's performance could be affected by a number of factors, including tiredness, anxiety or illness.

Normative assessment should always be supported by other techniques, in particular by observations: observing is an essential skill for everyone working with babies and children. At the end of each age section in the book are suggested activities which you can use to promote children's all-round development, and many of these also lend themselves to planned observations.

Reviewing development

This book also covers the current methods of reviewing development in child health clinics in the UK, and provides a useful guide to ways of stimulating development in children who have special needs. A useful list of resources and a comprehensive glossary are also included.

Chapter 1
Aspects of holistic child development

It is important to keep in mind that even a tiny baby is a person. 'Holistic development' sees the child in the round, as a whole person – physically, emotionally, intellectually, socially, morally, culturally and spiritually.

Learning about child development involves studying *patterns* of growth and development, from which guidelines for 'normal' development are drawn up.

Developmental **norms** are sometimes called *milestones* – they describe the recognised pattern of development that children are expected to follow. Each child will develop in a *unique* way, however: using norms helps in understanding these general patterns of development whilst recognising the wide variation between individuals.

Based on children growing up in Western Europe, the norms described in this book show what *most* children can do at particular stages.

Areas of development

The areas of development used in this book are these:

- *physical development*, including *sensory* development
- *cognitive and language development*
- *emotional and social development*
- *moral and spiritual development*.

Physical development

Physical development is the way in which the body increases in skill and becomes more complex in its performance. There are two main areas:

- **Gross motor skills** These use the large muscles in the body, and include walking, running, climbing and the like.
- **Fine motor skills** These include gross skills and fine skills.
  - **Gross manipulative skills** involve single limb movements, usually of the arm, for example throwing, catching, and making sweeping arm movements.
  - **Fine manipulative skills** involve precise use of the hands and fingers, for example pointing, drawing, using a knife and fork or chopsticks, writing, or doing up shoelaces.

Sensory development

Physical development also includes *sensory* development. **Sensation** is the process by which we receive information through the senses:

- vision
- hearing
- smell
- touch
- taste
- proprioception.

Proprioception is the sense that tells people where the mobile parts of their body, such as the legs, are in relation to the rest of the body.

Cognitive and language development

Cognitive or **intellectual** development is development of the mind – the part of the brain that is used for recognising, reasoning, knowing and understanding.

Perception involves people making sense of what they see, hear, touch, smell and taste. Perception is affected by previous experience and knowledge, and by the person's emotional state at the time.

Language development

Language development is the development of **communication** skills. These include skills in:

- **receptive speech** – what a person understands
- **expressive speech** – the words the person produces
- **articulation** – the person's actual pronunciation of words.

Emotional and social development

Emotional development

Emotional development involves the development of feelings:

- the growth of feelings about, and awareness of, *oneself*
- the development of feelings towards *other people*
- the development of **self-esteem** and a **self-concept**.

Social development

Social development includes the growth of the child's relationships with other people. **Socialisation** is the process of learning the skills and attitudes that enable the child to live easily with other members of the community.

Moral and spiritual development

Moral and spiritual development consists in a developing awareness of how to relate to others ethically, morally and humanely. It involves understanding values such as honesty and respect, and acquiring **concepts** such as right and wrong, and responsibility for the consequences of one's actions.

The pattern of development

Children's development follows a pattern:

➤ *From simple to complex*

Development progresses from simple actions to more complex ones. For example, children stand before they can walk, and walk before they can skip or hop.

➤ *From head to toe*

Development progresses downwards. Physical control and co-ordination begins with a child's head and develops down the body through the arms, hands and back, and finally to the legs and feet.

➤ From inner to outer

Development progresses from actions nearer the body to more complex ones further from the body. For example, children can co-ordinate their arms, using gross motor skills to reach for an object, before they have learned the fine motor skills necessary to use their fingers to pick it up.

➤ From general to specific

Development progresses from general responses to specific ones. For example, a young baby shows pleasure by a massive general response – the eyes widen, and the legs and arms move vigorously – whereas an older child shows pleasure by smiling or using appropriate words or gestures.

The various aspects of development are intricately linked: each affects and is affected by the others. For example, once children have reached the stage of emotional development at which they feel secure when apart from their main carer, they will have access to a much wider range of relationships, experiences and opportunities for learning. Similarly, when children can use language effectively, they will have more opportunities for social interaction. If one aspect is hampered or neglected in some way, children will be challenged in reaching their full potential.

Chapter 2
At birth

Newborn babies are already actively using all their senses to explore their new environment. They are seeing new things, listening to new sounds, and smelling new odours.

When not asleep, they are alert. Already they are learning to cope with a huge amount of new information.

Newborn babies can focus on objects less than one metre away. They show a marked preference for human faces.

They can recognise their mother's voice, and are settling into the world of noise, light, smell, taste and touch outside the womb.

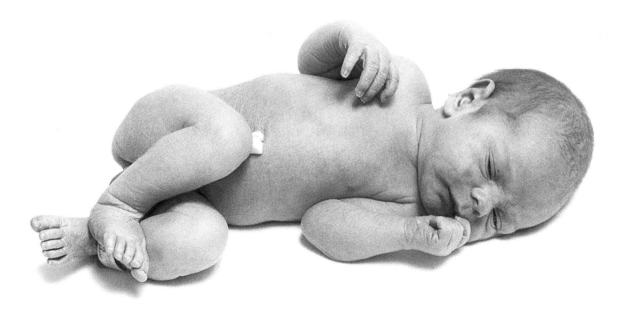

Physical development

Gross motor skills

Babies:

- lie **supine** (on their backs), with the head to one side.

Other physical positions are also characteristic:

- When placed on their front (the **prone** position), babies lie with the head turned to one side, the buttocks humped up and the knees tucked under the abdomen.

- When pulled to a sitting position, the head lags.

- When held up by a hand under the chest (**ventral suspension**), the head drops below the plane of the body, and the arms and legs are partly bent (**flexed**).

Fine motor skills

Babies:

- usually hold their hands tightly closed, but the hands may open spontaneously during feeding or when the back of the hand is stroked

- often hold their thumbs tucked in under their fingers.

Ventral suspension

Sensory development

Babies:

- will turn their head towards the light and will stare at bright, shiny objects

- are fascinated by human faces and gaze attentively at their carer's face when being fed or cuddled

- open their eyes when held upright

- close their eyes tightly if a pencil light is shone directly into them

- are known to like looking at high-contrast patterns and shapes

- blink in response to sound or movement

- are startled by sudden noises

- recognise their mother's or main carer's voice, at less than one week old

- cannot hear very soft sounds

- if breastfed, can distinguish the smell of their mother's breasts from those of other women who are breastfeeding

- show a preference for sweet tastes over salty, sour tastes

- are sensitive to textures and to any change of position

- have sensitive skin but may not respond to a very light touch.

Gazing at the carer's face

Reflexes of a newborn baby

Babies display a number of automatic movements, known as **primitive reflexes**, which are reflex responses to specific stimuli. These movements are inborn.

At about three months, the primitive reflexes are replaced by voluntary responses as the brain takes control of behaviour – for example, the grasp reflex has to fade before babies can learn to hold objects placed in their hands.

Primitive reflexes are important indicators of the health of the nervous system of babies. If they persist beyond an expected time, this may indicate a delay in development.

➤ *The swallowing and sucking reflexes*

When anything is put in the mouth, babies at once suck and swallow. Some babies while still in the womb make their fingers sore by sucking them.

➤ *The rooting reflex*

If one side of a baby's cheek or mouth is gently touched, the baby's head turns towards the touch and the mouth purses as if in search of the nipple.

The rooting reflex

➤ *The grasp reflex*

When an object or a finger touches the palm of the baby's hand, the hand automatically grasps it.

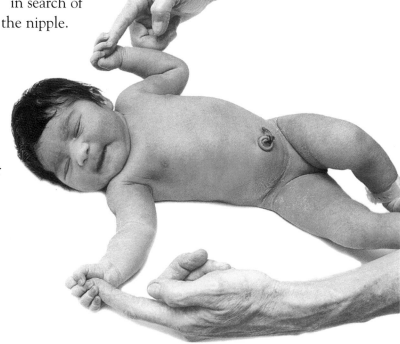

The grasp reflex

➤ The stepping or walking reflex

When held upright and tilting slightly forward, with their feet placed on a firm surface, babies will make forward-stepping movements.

➤ The asymmetric tonic neck reflex

If the baby's head is turned to one side, the baby will **extend** the arm and leg on that side and bend the arm and leg on the opposite side.

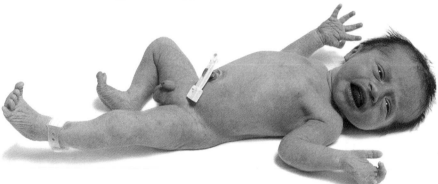

The stepping or walking reflex

➤ The startle reflex

When babies are startled by a sudden loud noise or bright light, they will move their arms outwards with elbows bent and hands clenched.

The asymmetric tonic neck reflex

➤ The falling reflex (Moro reflex)

Any sudden movement that affects the neck gives babies the feeling that they may be dropped; they will fling out the arms and open the hands, before bringing them back over the chest as if to catch hold of something.

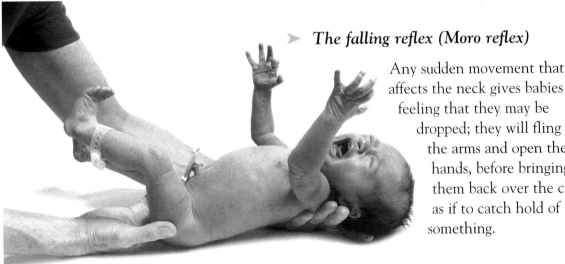

The falling reflex

Cognitive and language development

Babies:

- are beginning to develop concepts – concepts are abstract ideas, based in the senses and combined with growing understanding (for example, babies become aware of physical sensations such as hunger, and respond by crying)

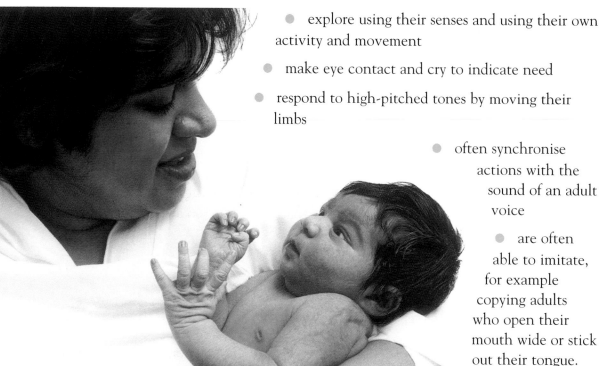

- explore using their senses and using their own activity and movement

- make eye contact and cry to indicate need

- respond to high-pitched tones by moving their limbs

- often synchronise actions with the sound of an adult voice

- are often able to imitate, for example copying adults who open their mouth wide or stick out their tongue.

Making eye contact

Emotional and social development

Babies:

- use total body movements to express pleasure at bathtime or when being fed

- enjoy feeding and cuddling

- often imitate facial expressions.

Play

Newborn babies respond to things that they see, hear and feel. Play might include the following.

➤ *Pulling faces*

Try sticking out your tongue and opening your mouth wide – the baby may copy you.

➤ *Showing objects*

Try showing the baby brightly coloured woolly pompoms, balloons, shiny objects, and black and white patterns. Hold the object directly in front of the baby's face, and give the baby time to focus on it. Then slowly move it.

➤ *Taking turns*

Talk with babies. If you talk to babies and leave time for a response, you will find that very young babies react, first with a concentrated expression and later with smiles and excited leg kicking.

Promoting development

- Provide plenty of physical contact, and maintain eye contact.
- Massage their body and limbs during or after bathing.
- Talk lovingly to babies and give them the opportunity to respond.
- Pick babies up and talk to them face to face.
- Encourage babies to lie on the floor and kick and experiment safely with movement.
- Provide opportunities for them to feel the freedom of moving without a nappy or clothes on.
- Use bright, contrasting colours in furnishings.
- Feed babies on demand, and talk and sing to them.
- Introduce them to different household noises.
- Provide contact with other adults and children.

- Encourage **bonding** with the baby's main carers by allowing time for them to enjoy the relationship.

- Expect no set routine within the first few weeks.

- Provide a mobile over the cot and/or the nappy-changing area.

- Light rattles and toys strung over the pram or cot will encourage focusing and co-ordination.

A mobile

Safety points

When playing with babies, always support the head – babies' neck muscles are not yet strong enough to control movement.

Never leave babies with a feeding bottle propped in their mouth.

Always place babies on their back to sleep.

Keep the temperature in a baby's room at around 20°C (68°F).

Activities

> *Design a mobile*

Ideas for students

1 Think of two or more designs for the mobile. (You could use a coat hanger or a cardboard tube as your basic structure.)

2 Compare your ideas, considering the following factors:
- availability of resources and materials
- skills and time required

- costs of materials
- appropriateness of the design for its purpose
- safety.

3 Select one of the designs and make the mobile.

You could use this activity in preparation for a child observation.

1 First, write down your instructions for making the mobile.

2 Now evaluate them: were they easy to follow, or did you have to modify the original plan?

3 Next, observe a baby reacting to the mobile, and record a detailed observation.

4 Did the baby react as you would expect for a baby of this age and stage of development?

➤ Contrast cards

1 Babies love to look at high-contrast black-and-white patterns. To encourage visual development, make some cards with different black and white patterns.

2 Attach the cards securely to the inside of the baby's pram or cot.

Chapter 3
One month

By 1 month, babies are beginning to smile in response to adult smiles. Their cries become more expressive, and they make non-crying noises such as cooing and gurgling.

They enjoy kicking their legs and waving their arms about.

They may imitate facial expressions, and are able to follow moving objects with their eyes.

Physical development

Gross motor skills

Babies:

- keep their head to one side when lying on their back (supine), with the arm and the leg on the face side outstretched, the knees apart, and the soles of the feet turned inwards

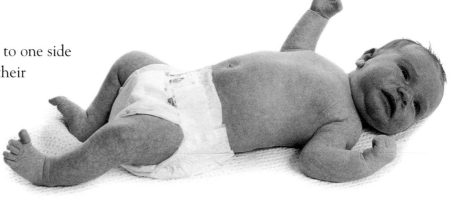

The supine position

- can turn from their side to their back

- will lift their head briefly from the prone position

- when held in ventral suspension, will keep the head in line with the body and the hips semi-extended

- make jerky and uncontrolled arm and leg movements

- if pulled to a sitting position, will show head lag

- are beginning to take their fists to their mouth

- open their hands from time to time.

Ventral suspension

Fine motor skills

Babies:

- show interest and excitement by their facial expressions
- open their hands to grasp an adult's finger.

Sensory development

Babies:

- focus their gaze at 20–25 cm (8–10 inches)
- turn their head towards a diffuse light source, and stare at bright shiny objects
- may move their head towards the source of a sound, but are not yet able to locate the sound
- are startled by sudden noises – when hearing a particular sound, they may momentarily 'freeze'

Turning towards a diffuse light source

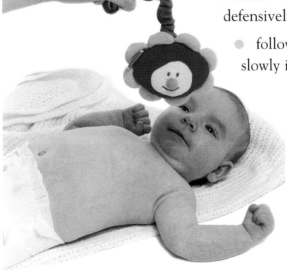

- blink defensively when something comes towards them
- follow the movement of a bright, dangling toy moved slowly in their line of vision – this is known as **tracking**.

Tracking a toy

Cognitive and language development

Babies:

- recognise their primary carers and show this by responding to them with a combination of excited movements, coos and smiles

- begin to repeat enjoyable movements, such as thumb-sucking

- make non-crying noises, such as cooing and gurgling

- cry in more expressive ways

- interact with an adult holding them up face-to-face, by simultaneously looking, listening, vocalising, and moving their arms and legs excitedly.

Emotional and social development

Babies:

- smile in response to an adult

- gaze attentively at the adult's face when being fed

- are beginning to show a particular **temperament** – for example placid or excitable

- enjoy sucking

- turn to regard a nearby speaker's face.

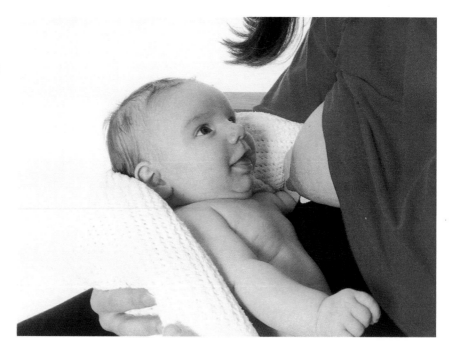

Gazing while being fed

Play

Babies:

- love to watch movement such as trees in the wind, or moving bright, contrasting objects placed within their field of vision
- enjoy listening to the sound of bells, music and voices, and rhythmic sounds.

Promoting development

- Use a special supporting infant chair so that babies can see adult activity.
- Let them kick freely without a nappy on.
- Massage the baby's body and limbs during or after bathing.
- Use brightly coloured mobiles and wind chimes over the baby's cot and/or changing mat.
- Encourage focusing and co-ordination by hanging light rattles and toys over the pram or cot.
- Talk to and smile with the baby.
- Sing while feeding or bathing the baby. Allow time for the baby to respond.
- Learn to differentiate between the baby's cries, and to respond to them appropriately.
- Encourage laughter by tickling the baby.
- Hold the baby close to promote a feeling of security.
- Try tying a few small bells safely around the baby's wrists. This encourages babies to watch their hands.

Safety points

Never leave rattles or similar toys in a baby's cot or pram. They could become wedged in the baby's mouth and might cause suffocation.

Do not leave a baby unattended on a table, work surface, bed or sofa. Lie the baby on the floor instead.

Activities

➤ *Following movement*

At around 6–10 weeks, babies begin to follow movement with their eyes. One way of promoting visual development – and of improving head–eye co-ordination – in young babies is to let the baby watch a moving toy.

1   Select a favourite toy – perhaps a teddy or a brightly coloured toy.

2   Hold the toy about 1 metre (3 feet) in front of the baby.

3   Slowly move the toy from side to side so that the baby's eyes can follow it.

4   As the baby gets better at following the movement, swing the toy farther each way.

5   Try different directions – up and down, towards and away from the baby.

Idea for students

You could write a detailed observation of the activity.

➤ *Baby massage*

Massage has many benefits for a baby. It is very soothing and can calm a fretful baby. It is also a very good way of showing love.

The main points to remember are that the experience should:

- benefit both the baby and the carer, creating a feeling of calm and increasing the carer's confidence in handling techniques
- be conducted in a relaxed atmosphere, avoiding distractions such as the telephone or other people
- always be symmetrical – both sides of the baby's body should be massaged at the same time
- take place in a warm room
- be an unhurried, relaxing experience.

The following is an appropriate massage sequence.

1   Prepare the room by making sure that there are no draughts and that the room is warm. Remove any jewellery and make sure that your nails have no rough edges.

2   You could use a mat with a thick towel on the floor, or simply lie the baby along your lap – make sure your own back is supported.

3   Use a baby oil. Warm it by first rubbing it between your palms.

4   Work down from the baby's head, using a light, circular motion. First massage the crown of the baby's head *very gently*; then move on to the forehead, cheeks and ears.

5   Gently massage the baby's neck, from the ears down to the shoulders, and from the chin to the chest.

6   Gently stroke the baby's arms, starting from the shoulders and going all the way to the fingertips.

7   Stroke down the baby's chest and tummy, rubbing in a circular direction.

8   Gently massage the baby's legs, from the thighs to the ankles.

9   Massage the baby's feet, stroking from heel to toe. Concentrate on each toe individually.

10 Finally, turn the baby over onto the front and gently massage the back.

Throughout the procedure, talk softly to the baby and always leave one hand in contact with the baby's body, to provide security and comfort.

Chapter 4
Three months

By 3 months, babies are showing more interest in playthings.

They like to kick vigorously and to clasp their hands together.

They respond to familiar situations by a combination of excited movements, smiles and a variety of vocalisations, such as cries, cooing sounds and chuckles.

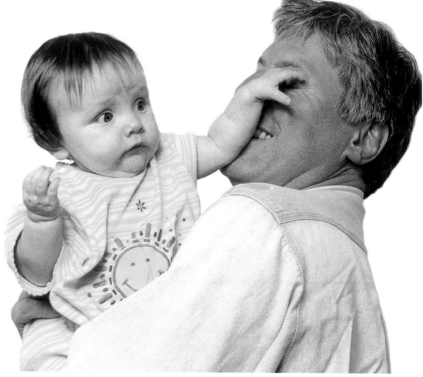

Physical development

Gross motor skills

Babies:

- keep their head in a central position when lying supine

- can now lift both their head and their chest off the bed in the prone position, supported on their forearms

Lifting the head and chest in the prone position

- when held in ventral suspension, keep their head above the line of the body

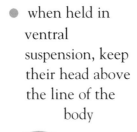

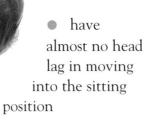

- have almost no head lag in moving into the sitting position

Raised head in ventral suspension

Little head lag while being pulled to a sitting position

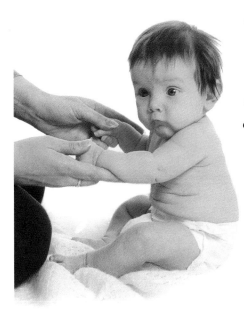

- when held, can sit with their back straight

- kick vigorously, with their legs alternating or occasionally together

- can wave their arms and bring their hands together over their body.

Fine motor skills

Babies:

- move their head to follow adults' movements

- watch their hands and play with their fingers

- clasp and unclasp their hands at the midline of the body, and take them to their mouth

Straight back when sitting

- can hold a rattle for a brief time before dropping it.

Sensory development

Babies:

- are able to focus their eyes on the same point

- can move their head deliberately to gaze around them

- prefer moving objects to still ones – their eyes will follow a moving toy from side to side (through 180°)

- turn their eyes towards a sound source, especially a human voice

Playing with the hands and fingers

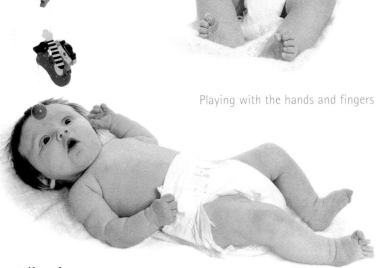

Eyes following a moving toy

- respond to their name being called

- often suck their lips in response to the sounds of food preparation

- are distressed by sudden loud noises

- are fascinated by human faces and can recognise their mother's or main carer's face in a photograph.

Cognitive and language development

Babies:

- take an increasing interest in their surroundings

- laugh and vocalise, with increasing tone and intensity

- are becoming conversational by cooing, gurgling and chuckling – they can exchange coos with familiar person

- smile in response to speech

- show an increasing interest in playthings

- cry loudly when expressing a need

- understand cause and effect – for example, if you tie one end of a ribbon to their toe and the other to a mobile, they will learn to move the mobile.

Emotional and social development

Babies:

- show enjoyment at caring routines such as bathtime

- respond with obvious pleasure to loving attention and cuddles

- fix their eyes unblinkingly on the carer's face when feeding

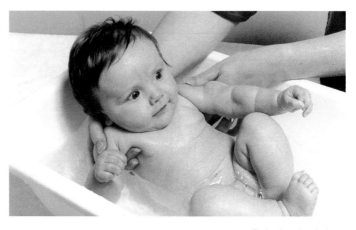

Enjoying bathtime

- stay awake for longer periods of time (70 per cent of babies at this age sleep through the night)
- smile at familiar people and at strangers.

Play

Babies:

- enjoy holding rattles, chiming balls and musical toys
- love to explore different textures, for example on an activity mat.

Responding with pleasure to being cuddled

Promoting development

- Use a supporting infant chair so that the baby can watch adult activity.
- Provide brightly coloured mobiles and wind chimes to encourage focusing at 20 cm (8 inches).
- Place some toys on a blanket or play mat on the floor. Let the baby lie on her or his tummy and play with the toys for short periods.
- Give the baby a rattle to hold.
- Attach objects above the cot which make a noise when touched.
- Imitate the sounds made by the baby and encourage repetition.
- Sing nursery rhymes.
- Change the baby's position frequently so that there are different things to look at and to experience.
- Encourage contact with other adults and children.

- Try action rhymes with the baby on your lap, such as 'This little piggy went to market ...'.

- Respond to the baby's needs and show enjoyment in providing care.

- Tickle the baby to provide enjoyment.

- Massage or stroke the baby's limbs when bathing or if using massage oil.

Safety points

Always protect babies, of *all* skin tones, from exposure to sunlight. Use a special sun-protection cream, a sun hat to protect the face and neck, and a pram canopy.

Never leave small objects within reach – everything finds its way to a baby's mouth.

When you buy goods, always check for an appropriate safety symbol.

Activities

➤ **A *simple game or toy***

Design and make a simple game or toy that will encourage a baby's sensory development.

1 Think about the stage of development the child has reached. Plan to make a game or toy that will promote development of one or more of the baby's senses – examples are an activity mat, sound lotto, a 'feely' bag, or a game of matching smells.

2 Points to consider are:
   - safety
   - hygiene
   - suitability for the purpose.

Ideas for students

You could use this activity for a child observation.

1 First, say which sense you hope your game or toy will develop, and describe how it will help.

2 Next, observe a baby playing with the game or toy, and record a detailed observation.

3   Did the baby react as you would expect for a baby of this age and stage of development?

➤ *A secret mirror table*

Mirrors are a good way to promote visual awareness: they catch the light and reflect different colours, and babies can also see their own movements reflected.

1   Stick a few mirror tiles to the underside of a low table.

2   Place the baby underneath the table so that she or he can look up into the mirror tiles. Check that there is enough light.

3   Try to provide a contrasting image – for instance, if the baby's clothing is pale, place the baby on a dark sheet.

Safety point

Before placing the baby on the floor, make sure that there are no draughts.

Chapter 5
Six months

By 6 months, babies are able to reach for and grab things with both hands. They extend their exploration by using their hands to touch, stroke and pat. Most toys are transferred to the mouth.

They love to imitate sounds and enjoy babbling.

They continue to find other people fascinating, but are wary of strangers.

Physical development

Gross motor skills

Babies:

Using the hands and arms for support

- if lying on their back can roll over, moving from their back to their stomach

- if lying on their stomach can lift their head and chest, supporting themselves on their arms and hands

- can use their shoulders to pull themselves into a sitting position

Using the shoulders while moving to a sitting position

- can bear almost all their own weight

- when held standing, do so with a straight back

Bearing most of the weight

- when held sitting, do so with a straight back

- when held on the floor, bounce their feet up and down

- lift their legs into a vertical position and grasp one or both feet with their hands

Sitting with a straight back

Grasping the feet with the hands

- kick vigorously with their legs alternating

- move their arms purposefully and hold them up, indicating a wish to be lifted

- change the angle of their body to reach out for an object.

Fine motor skills

Babies:

- reach and grab when a small toy is offered

- use their whole hand (**palmar grasp**) to pass a toy from one hand to the other

Using a palmar grasp

- poke at small objects with their index finger
- explore objects by putting them in their mouth.

Sensory development

Babies:

- adjust their position to see objects
- are visually very alert, and follow another child's or an adult's activities across the room with increased alertness
- turn towards the source when they hear sounds at ear level.

Exploring objects with the mouth

Cognitive and language development

Babies:

- understand the meaning of words such as 'bye-bye', 'mama' or 'dada'
- understand objects and know what to expect of them – given a can that makes a noise, for instance, they will test it for other unexpected behaviour
- turn immediately when they hear mother's or main carer's voice at a distance
- show some understanding of the emotional state of their mother's or main carer's voice
- understand 'up' and 'down' and make appropriate gestures, such as raising their arms to be picked up
- babble spontaneously, using first monosyllables such as 'ga, ga' and then double syllables such as 'goo-ga', and later combining vowels and consonants
- talk to themselves in a tuneful, sing-song voice
- squeal with delight.

Emotional and social development

Babies:

- manage to feed themselves using their fingers
- offer toys to others
- are more wary of strangers
- show distress when their mother leaves
- are more aware of other people's feelings, crying if a sibling cries, for example, or laughing when others do – this is called *recognising an emotion*: it does not mean that they are *really* laughing or crying.

Play

Babies:

- show delight in response to active play
- enjoy playing with stacking beakers and bricks
- love to explore objects with both their hands and their mouth
- play with a rolling ball when in a sitting position.

Promoting development

- Encourage confidence and balance by placing toys around the sitting baby.

Delighting in active play

Chapter 6
Nine months

Babies enjoy exploring their environment by crawling or shuffling on their bottoms.

They often bounce in time to music and take pleasure in songs and action rhymes. They can sit, lean forward and pull objects towards them.

Babies understand their daily routine and like to imitate adult speech and gestures.

Physical development

Gross motor skills

Babies:

- can maintain a sitting position with a straight back

- can sit unsupported for up to 15 minutes

- turn their body to look sideways when stretching out to pick up a toy from the floor

- pull themselves to a standing position, but are unable to lower themselves and tend to fall backwards with a bump

- stand holding onto furniture

- find ways of moving about the floor – for example by rolling, wriggling, or crawling on their stomach

Sits alone playing with toy

- may take some steps when both hands are held.

Attempting to crawl

Fine motor skills

Babies:

- manipulate toys by passing them from one hand to the other

- can grasp objects between finger and thumb in a **pincer grip**

- can release a toy from their grasp by dropping it, but cannot yet put it down voluntarily

- move arms up and down together when excited.

Grasping an object using a pincer grip

Cognitive and language development

Babies:

- can judge the size of an object up to 60 cm (2 feet) away
- look in the correct direction for fallen toys
- watch a toy being hidden and then look for it – this shows that they know that an object can exist even when it is no longer in sight (**object permanence**)
- recognise familiar pictures
- understand their daily routine and will follow simple instructions such as 'kiss teddy'
- use an increasing variety of intonation when babbling
- enjoy communicating with sounds
- imitate adult sounds, like a cough or a 'brrr' noise
- understand and obey the command 'no'
- know general characteristics of their language – for example, they can distinguish English from Polish.

Hiding an object ...

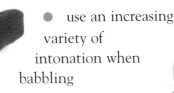

... and 'finding' it again

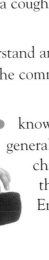

Emotional and social development

Babies:

- enjoy songs and action rhymes

- still prefer to be near to a familiar adult

- play alone for long periods

- show definite likes and dislikes at meals and at bedtimes

- often need to have a **comfort object**, such as a blanket or a favourite teddy

- still take everything to the mouth

- may drink from a cup with help

- enjoy pointing at objects

- enjoy making noises by banging toys.

Taking things to the mouth

Play

Playing alone

Babies:

- play alone for long periods

- enjoy making noises by banging toys

- like to play with empty cardboard boxes.

Promoting development

- Allow plenty of time for play.

- Encourage mobility by placing toys just out of reach.

- Provide small objects for babies to pick up – choose objects that are safe when chewed, such as pieces of biscuit – but always supervise them.

- Provide bath toys such as beakers, sponges and funnels.

- Provide stacking and nesting toys.

- Play peek-a-boo games, and hide-and-seek.

- Roll balls for the baby to bring back to you.

- Encourage self-feeding and tolerate messes.

- Talk constantly to babies, and continue with rhymes and action songs.

Exploring a picture book

Safety points

Always supervise eating and drinking. Never leave babies alone with finger foods such as bananas, carrots, or cheese.

Use child-proof containers for tablets and vitamins. Ensure that the containers are closed properly.

Use a locked cupboard for storing dangerous household chemicals such as bleach, disinfectant and white spirit.

Activities

➤ *A game of hide-and-seek*

1   Choose one of the baby's favourite playthings – perhaps a small soft toy or rattle.

2   Place the baby in a sitting position or lying on his or her stomach.

3   While the baby is watching, place the toy in full view and within easy reach. The baby may reach for the object.

4 Still in full view of the baby, partly cover the toy with a cloth, so that only part of it is visible. Again, the baby may reach for the toy.

5 While the baby is reaching for the toy, cover the toy completely with the cloth. Does the baby continue to reach for it?

6 While the baby is still interested in the toy, and again in full view of the baby, completely cover the toy with the cloth once more. Notice whether the baby tries to pull the cloth away or to search for the toy in some way.

Ideas for students

Games of hide-and-seek indicate whether the baby has developed the concept of object permanence. You could explore this in a child observation. You will need to find a baby aged between 6 months and a year whose parent is happy for you to try this activity.

1 Follow the procedure outlined above. At each stage, note whether the baby reaches for the toy.

2 Write up the results of the activity in the form of an observation.

3 If possible, compare this observation with observations of other children.

Research shows that step **4** – continuing to reach for the partly-covered toy – is typically experienced at about 6 months; step **5** at about 7 months; and step **6** at about 8 months.

Chapter 7
Twelve months

The way babies view their world changes dramatically as they begin to be more mobile, crawling rapidly or cruising along and using the furniture for support.

At 12 months they are usually still shy with strangers. Often they have a favourite comfort object, such as a teddy or a cloth.

Language develops into a conversation, with increasing intonation, although there are very few recognisable words.

They are developing their own sense of identity.

Physical development

Gross motor skills

Babies:

- can rise to a sitting position from lying down

- can rise to standing without help from furniture or people

- can stand alone for a few moments

- can crawl on their hands and knees, bottom-shuffle, or use their hands and feet to move rapidly about the floor ('bear-walking')

- can 'cruise' along using furniture as a support

- can probably walk alone, with their feet wide apart and their arms raised to maintain balance – or walk with one hand held.

By 13 months, babies:

- can often walk (about 50 per cent of babies walk by this age), but tend to fall over frequently and sit down rather suddenly.

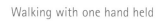

Walking with one hand held

By 15 months, babies:

- crawl upstairs safely and may come downstairs backwards

- are generally able to walk alone

- kneel without support.

Walking alone, with feet apart

Fine motor skills

Babies:

- can pick up small objects with a fine pincer grip, between the thumb and the tip of the index finger

- can point with the index finger at objects of interest

- can release a small object into someone's hand

- can hold a crayon in a palmar grasp, and turn several pages of a book at once

- show a preference for one hand over the other, but use either

Showing a preference for one hand over the other

- drop and throw toys deliberately – and look to see where they have fallen

- build with a few bricks and arrange toys on the floor.

By 15 months, babies:

- can put small objects into a bottle

- can grasp a crayon with either hand in a palmar grasp, and imitate to-and-fro scribble

- may build a tower of two cubes after this has been demonstrated.

Sensory development

Babies:

- can see almost as well as an adult – their visual memory is very good: they may find things that an adult has mislaid

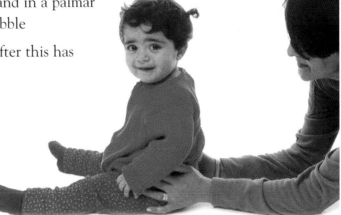

Turning in response to hearing her own name

- know and respond immediately to their own name, and recognise familiar sounds and voices

- stroke, pat and turn objects in their hands, and recognise familiar objects by touch alone
- discriminate between different foods by taste, and show a preference for sweet, salt and fatty flavours
- often enjoy watching television.

By 15 months, babies:

- demand objects out of reach by pointing with their index finger
- point to familiar people, animals or toys when requested.

Cognitive and language development

Babies:

- use trial-and-error methods to learn about objects
- understand simple instructions associated with a gesture, such as 'come to Daddy', 'clap hands', and 'wave bye-bye'
- both point and look to where others point, which implies some understanding of how others see and think
- speak 2–6 or more recognisable words and show that they understand many more – babbling has developed into a much more speech-like form, with increased intonation
- hand objects to adults when asked, and begin to treat objects in an appropriate way, for example cuddle a teddy but use a hairbrush.

Using a hairbrush

Deaf babies stop babbling at around the age of 12 months because they begin to learn the special manual gestures of sign language.

By 15 months, babies:

- understand the names of various parts of the body
- identify pictures of a few named objects

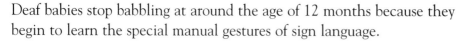

- understand 'no', 'show me' and 'look'

- watch where objects fall, and can seek out a hidden toy

- move one object to reach another that was hidden from view.

Seeing a toy and a beaker together ...

... recognising that the hidden toy may be with the beaker ...

... and finding the toy

Emotional and social development

Babies:

- are emotionally **labile** – that is, they are likely to have fluctuating moods
- are closely dependent upon an adult's reassuring presence
- often want a comfort object, such as a teddy or a piece of cloth
- are still shy with strangers
- are affectionate towards familiar people
- enjoy socialising at mealtimes, joining in conversations while mastering the task of self-feeding
- help with daily routines, such as getting washed and dressed
- play pat-a-cake and wave good-bye, both spontaneously and on request.

By 15 months, babies:

- repeatedly throw objects to the floor in play or rejection (this is known as **casting**)
- carry dolls or teddies by their limbs, hair or clothing.

Play

Babies:

- enjoy playing with bricks, and with containers – they put toys into them and then take them out
- love to play with toys that they can move along with their feet
- enjoy looking at picture books.

Promoting development

- Provide a wheeled push-and-pull toy to promote confidence in walking.
- Provide stacking toys and bricks.

- Read picture books with simple rhymes.

- Arrange a corner of the kitchen or garden for messy play. Encourage the use of water, play dough or paint.

- Encourage skills of **creativity** by providing thick crayons and paint brushes and large sheets of paper (such as wall lining paper).

- Play simple games with the baby which involve action and taking turns, such as the 'hand sandwich' game.

- Join in games of 'let's pretend' to encourage skills of **imagination** – for example, pretending to be animals or to drive a bus.

- Encourage **role-play** games of make-believe – for example, pretending to be a doctor, a vet or a superhero.

- Talk to the baby about everyday activities, but always allow time for a response.

- Provide an interesting, varied environment, which contains pictures, music, books and food all of which stimulate the senses.

- Consider attending a mother-and-toddler group or a similar group.

Playing a 'hand sandwich' game

Safety points

As babies become more mobile, you need to be vigilant at all times. This is a very high-risk age for accidents.

Always supervise sand and water play.

Use safety equipment such as safety catches for cupboards and stair gates, ideally at the top and bottom of stairs.

Activities

➤ *A pull-along snake*

Once a child is walking with confidence, you could make a colourful pull-along toy. Brightly painted cotton reels threaded onto soft cord or string make an attractive 'snake' for children to pull along. Alternatively, you could thread together plastic hair rollers or large round beads.

1   Paint 10–12 large cotton reels in bright colours, using lead-free paint.

2   Thread the reels onto a cord, about 0.75 m (20 inches) long.

3   Make sure the reels are about 0.5 cm (¹/₄ inch) apart, so that the snake will twist and turn when pulled.

4   Use a large oval bead to make the snake's head. Paint an eye on each side.

5   Use small wooden or plastic beads to make an easy-to-grip handle.

This activity promotes the motor skills of balance and co-ordination, and encourages children to become aware of their ability to control their own environment.

➤ *Choosing toys for babies*

Visit a toyshop and look at the range of toys for babies under 18 months old. Make a list – you could group the toys and activities under two headings:

● toys that will strengthen muscles and improve co-ordination skills

● toys that will particularly stimulate the senses of touch, hearing and sight.

Check the safety symbols shown on the toys.

Ideas for students

If you were asked to suggest toys and activities for a baby with visual impairment, what specific toys could you suggest? Why?

Chapter 8
Eighteen months

Children of 18 months enjoy being able to walk well and to climb up and down stairs with help.

They can pick up small objects with a delicate pincer grasp, and show a preference for using one hand.

They enjoy simple picture books, and they can understand and obey simple commands.

They have an increasing desire for independence, and are developing a recognisable character and **personality** of their own.

Physical development

Children:

- can walk steadily and stop safely, without sitting down suddenly

- can climb forward into an adult chair and then turn round and sit

Walking steadily – even while carrying a toy

Climbing onto an adult chair...

... and turning around to sit on it

- can kneel upright without support

- can squat to pick up a toy

- can move without support from a squatting position to standing

Squatting to pick up a toy

- can climb up stairs and down stairs if their hand is held or using a rail for balance – they put two feet on each step before moving on to the next step

- can crawl backwards (on their stomachs) down stairs alone

- can run steadily but are unable to avoid obstacles in their path.

Fine motor skills: gross manipulative skills

Children:

- can point to known objects

- can build a tower of three or more bricks.

Crawling down stairs alone

Fine motor skills: fine manipulative skills

Children:

- can use a delicate pincer grasp to pick up very small objects

- can use a spoon when feeding themselves

- can hold a pencil, in their whole hand or between the thumb and the first two fingers (this is called the **primitive tripod grasp**)

- can scribble to and fro with a pencil on paper

- can thread large beads onto a lace or string

- can control their wrist movement to manipulate objects

- can remove small objects from a bottle by turning it upside-down.

Using a primitive tripod grasp

Children:

- recognise familiar people at a distance
- realise that they are looking at themselves in the mirror
- no longer take everything to their mouths to explore it.

Cognitive and language development

Children:

- know the names of parts of their bodies, and can point to them when asked
- use 6–40 recognisable words and understand many more – the word most often used is 'no'
- echo the last part of what others say (**echolalia**)
- over-extend words or signs, giving them several meanings (**holophrase**) – for example, 'cat' may be used to refer to *all* animals, not just cats
- begin waving their arms up and down, meaning 'Start again', 'More' or 'I like it'
- use **gestures** alongside words
- indicate desire by pointing, urgent vocalisations or words
- obey simple instructions such as 'Shut the door', and respond to simple questions such as 'Where's the pussy-cat?'
- enjoy trying to sing, as well as to listen to songs and rhymes
- refer to themselves by name
- recognise that people may have different desires (younger babies assume that everyone feels the same as they do).

Emotional and social development

Children:

- remember where objects belong (this reflects an increase in long-term memory)
- play contentedly alone (**solitary play**), but *prefer* to be near a familiar adult or sibling
- are eager to be independent, for example to dress themselves ('Me do it!')
- are aware that others are fearful or anxious for them as they climb on or off chairs, etc.
- alternate between clinging and resistance
- may easily become frustrated, with occasional temper tantrums
- may indicate toilet needs by restlessness or words
- can follow stories, and enjoy stories and rhymes that include repetition.

Playing contentedly alone

Play

Children:

- like things that screw and unscrew
- enjoy posting objects into boxes, as when posting letters
- like paints and crayons
- enjoy sand and water play, and associated toys
- like to play matching and sorting games, for example stacking beakers
- enjoy simple jigsaw puzzles
- love puppet play and action rhymes.

Playing with a finger puppet

Promoting development

- Continue to provide walker trucks, pull-along animals, and the like.
- Encourage play with messy materials, such as sand, water and play dough.
- Provide low, stable furniture to climb on.
- Provide pop-up toys, stacking toys and hammer-and-peg toys, which develop hand–eye co-ordination skills.
- Provide balls to roll, kick or throw.
- Provide toys that encourage make-believe play and language skills, such as simple puppets, dressing-up clothes, or toy telephones.
- Use action rhymes and singing games to promote conversation and confidence. Play with other children will help, too.
- Provide bath toys, such as simple beakers, sprinkling toys and waterproof books.
- Use finger-paints and wax crayons to encourage creative skills.
- Provide picture books, and encourage children to turn the pages and to identify details in the pictures.

Sharing an interactive activity

Safety points

Always supervise children in the bath. Never leave a child alone in the bath, even for a few minutes.

When children are climbing or playing outside, be aware of dangers such as sharp objects, litter or unfenced ponds.

Activities

➤ *A treasure chest*

Make a treasure chest for a child aged 18 months.

1 Use a strong, shallow cardboard box, an old solid wooden drawer, or a wicker basket.

2 Check that there are no staples, splinters or jagged edges.

3 Select a variety of interesting objects (about 10–15 in all) that will stimulate each of the child's senses – objects with different shapes, weights, colours and textures. You may also be able to include objects that have a distinctive smell, such as a small empty perfume bottle or a lavender bag.

A treasure chest

Ideas for students

You could use this activity for a child observation.

1 Sit to one side and observe the child playing alone with the contents of the treasure chest. Write a detailed, timed observation of the activity, including the following points:

- what the child does with each object
- how long he or she plays with each object
- what expressions or sounds he or she makes
- how involved he or she is in the activity.

2 Evaluate the activity in terms of its value to the child's overall development and enjoyment.

3 What would you change if you were to repeat the activity?

> *Puppet play*

Make two simple finger puppets: one (large) for you, and the other (slightly smaller) for the child.

1 Using a square of felt, cut and stick or sew a small cap shape to fit over the finger. Decorate it with hair (wool) and a face.

2 Play a game in which the child copies your actions, such as:

> *My little man bows down*
> *My little man turns round*
> *My little man jumps up and down*
> *And makes a funny sound – BOO!*

This activity promotes manipulative skills, social and language development, and the development of imagination.

Chapter 9
Two years

By 2 years, children can run, jump, kick, and use words as well as actions to express themselves.

They are curious and impulsive explorers of their environment, and want to be as independent as possible.

They easily become frustrated when they cannot express themselves or are prevented from doing something they want to do.

They may show strong emotions in 'temper tantrums' or bursting into tears – the classic 'terrible twos'. They are also affected by the emotions of others and will laugh or cry in sympathy.

Physical development

Gross motor skills

Children:

- can run safely, avoiding obstacles, and are very mobile

- can climb up onto furniture

- can throw a ball overhand, but cannot yet catch a ball

- push and pull large, wheeled toys

- walk up and down stairs, usually putting both feet on each step

- walk into a large ball when attempting to kick it

- sit on a tricycle and propel it with their feet – they cannot yet use the pedals

- squat with complete steadiness.

By 2¹/₂ years, children:

- stand on tiptoe when shown how to do this

- climb nursery apparatus

- jump with both feet together from a low step

- kick a large ball, but gently and lopsidedly.

Fine motor skills

Children:

- draw circles, lines and dots using their preferred hand
- pick up tiny objects using a fine pincer grasp
- can build a tower of six or more blocks, with a longer concentration span
- enjoy picture books and turn the pages singly
- can copy a vertical line and sometimes a 'V' shape
- can drink from a cup with fewer spills, and manage scooping with a spoon at mealtimes.

By 2½ years, children:

- can hold a pencil in their preferred hand, with an improved tripod grasp
- can build a tower of seven or more cubes, using their preferred hand
- can imitate a horizontal line, a circle, a 'T' and a 'V'.

Drinking confidently from a cup

Sensory development

Children:

- recognise familiar people in photographs after being shown them once, but do not yet recognise themselves in photographs
- listen to general conversation with interest.

By 2½ years, children:

- recognise themselves in photos
- recognise minute details in picture books.

Cognitive and language development

Children:

- are particularly interested in the names of people and objects

- are beginning to understand the consequences of their own actions and those of others, for example when something falls over or breaks

- provide comfort when other babies cry – **empathy** requires a deep knowledge of other minds (younger babies cry when others cry)

- talk to themselves often, but may not always be understood by others

- now speak over two hundred words, and accumulate new words very rapidly

- understand many more words than they can speak (possibly over a thousand)

- talk about an absent object when reminded of it – seeing an empty plate, for instance, they may say 'biscuit'

- often omit opening or closing consonants, so 'bus' may become 'us', or 'coat' become 'coa'

- use phrases as **telegraphic speech** (or **telegraphese**) – for example, 'daddy-car' might mean a number of different things, including 'Daddy's in his car', 'I want to go in Daddy's car' or 'Daddy's car is outside'

- spend a great deal of time in naming things and what they do, such as 'chair' or 'step' and 'up'

- follow simple instructions and requests, such as 'Please bring me the book'

- want to share songs, conversations and finger-rhymes more and more.

By 2½ years, children:

- know their full name

- still repeat words spoken to them (**echolalia**)

- continually ask questions beginning 'What … ?' or 'Who … ?'

- use the pronouns 'I', 'me' and 'you' correctly

- talk audibly and intelligibly to themselves when playing

- can say a few nursery rhymes.

Emotional and social development

Children:

- are beginning to express how they feel
- are impulsive and curious about their environment
- are eager to try out new experiences
- may be clingy and dependent at times, and self-reliant and independent at others
- often feel frustrated when unable to express themselves – about half of 2-year-old children have tantrums on a more or less daily basis
- can dress themselves and go to the toilet independently; but may need sensitive help with pulling their pants up
- often like to help others, but not when doing so conflicts with their own desires.

By 2½ years, children:

- eat skilfully with a spoon and may use a fork
- may be dry through the night (but there is wide variation)
- are emotionally still very dependent on an adult
- play more with other children, but may not share their toys with them.

Play

Children:

- love physical games, including running, jumping, climbing
- like to build with construction toys
- engage in more sustained role-play, such as putting dolls to bed or driving a car
- often play alone (solitary play) or watch other children playing (**spectator play**)

Spectator play

- may play alongside other children, but not with them (**parallel play**)

- enjoy playing **symbolically**, letting one thing stand for another (**pretend play**) – for example, children may pretend that they are tiny babies and crawl into a doll's bed, or push a block on the floor, pretending that it is a train: this rich **imaginative play** shows their minds at work and often reveals feelings that cannot be expressed in words

Parallel play

- enjoy helping around the house

- enjoy musical games.

Promoting development

- Provide toys to ride and climb on, and space to run and play.

- Encourage children to develop an interest in the natural world, including plants and wildlife.

- Encourage the use of safe climbing frames and sandpits, but always under supervision.

- Provide opportunities for messy play with water and paints.

- Encourage ball play (throwing and catching), to promote co-ordination skills.

- Provide bricks, sorting boxes, hammer-and-peg toys and simple jigsaw puzzles – these improve co-ordination and motor skills.

- Provide simple models to build (such as Duplo®).

- Provide picture books, crayons and paper, and glove puppets.

- Be relaxed about toilet training – always praise children when they succeed, and do not show disapproval when they do not.

- Help children to learn how to express their feelings in ways that are honest and open, but without hurting others.

- Provide play dough or soft clay. Encourage children to express their feelings – for instance, frustration can be expressed by pummelling and hitting the dough.

- Play simple games of 'Let's pretend'.

- Provide resources for role-play, including hats and clothes for dressing-up.

Safety points

Never leave children alone when playing with water or on outdoor play equipment. They are very adventurous, but do not yet have a strong enough sense of danger.

Make sure that any likely hiding places in the home or garden, such as cupboards and sheds, cannot be locked from the inside.

Activities

➤ *Finger-painting*

At first, painting is best done with the fingers as this frees children from having to control a brush, and allows direct contact between the textures of the paint and the children themselves.

1 Protect the area and the child's clothes.

2 Place a large sheet of paper on the floor or a table – lining paper or the wrong side of wallpaper are cheap sources.

3 Arrange the prepared paint colours in a palette or on plates. Stand these on the paper also.

4 Encourage the child to use all the colours, and to mix them and see how the colours change.

Finger-paints may be bought ready-made, or you can make your own. Mix together:

- $\frac{1}{2}$ cup of soap flakes – use *real* soap, not detergent

- $\frac{1}{2}$ cup of cold water starch

- $\frac{3}{4}$ cup of cold water

- food colourings.

This activity promotes the development of manipulative skills, and sensory, cognitive and language development.

➤ Modelling with play dough

Modelling or just manipulating play dough enables children to learn about different materials, gives scope to their imagination, and is a soothing and relaxing activity.

Try the play-dough recipe below – this dough lasts well when stored in a plastic bag or box in the fridge, and it has a good texture for young children to handle.

Play-dough recipe:

- 1 cup of water
- 1 tablespoon of cooking oil
- 1 heaped cup of plain flour
- 1 cup of salt
- 2 teaspoons of cream of tartar
- food colouring as required.

To make the play dough:

1 Mix the water, the oil and a few drops of food colouring in a pan. Heat gently.

2 Add the rest of the ingredients and stir.

3 The dough will start to form and will lift away from the pan. Turn off the heat. Remove the dough from the pan and leave it to cool.

Allow the child to handle the dough freely at first to explore the possibilities. Then you could provide a variety of tools for play cooking, for example shape cutters, a rolling pin, plastic knives, a spatula, and some small plastic bowls and plates.

Safety points

When making the dough you can let children help with the measuring, but take extreme care to keep the hot saucepan away from their reach.

Dough made according to the recipe above will last for up to a month if kept wrapped in the fridge. If using other recipes, follow the instructions for storage and use.

Make sure that children do not *eat* the dough – even commercially made play dough includes ordinary flour (about 40 per cent of the mixture). Extra vigilance is needed by staff to stop children with **coeliac disease** putting the dough into their mouth.

Chapter 10
Three years

Children now demonstrate that they have an inner world of thought and that they can also talk about this.

Their drawings and paintings are beginning to include recognisable representations of people and things.

They now play *with* other children rather than just *near* them, and are making their first friends.

Physical development

Gross motor skills

Children:

- can jump from a low step

- can walk backwards and sideways

- can stand and walk on tiptoe, and stand on one foot

- can ride a tricycle using pedals

- climb stairs with one foot on each step, and go downwards with two feet on each step

- have good spatial awareness – they can manoeuvre themselves around objects

- can throw a ball overhand, and can catch a large ball with arms outstretched

- use their whole body to kick a ball with force.

Jumping from the bottom stair

Using the pedals on a tricycle

Climbing stairs

Fine motor skills

Children:

- can build towers of nine or ten cubes
- can copy a building pattern of three or more cubes including a bridge
- can control a pencil using their thumb and the first two fingers (the **dynamic tripod grip**)

Building a tower of cubes

Copying a building pattern
including a bridge

- can copy a circle and the letters 'V', 'H' and 'T'
- enjoy standing at an easel and painting with a large brush
- can draw a person with head, and sometimes with legs and (later) arms coming out from the head – squiggles inside the head represent a face
- can cut paper with scissors
- can thread large beads onto a lace
- can eat using a fork or spoon.

Cutting paper with scissors

In China children of 3 years of age are able to eat with chopsticks, whereas the competent use of knives and forks in other cultures usually starts at age 5. It is thought that this cultural difference is due to early encouragement and a great deal of practice, rather than to a greater inborn manual dexterity.

Cognitive and language development

Children:

- can match two or three primary colours, usually red and yellow, but sometimes confuse blue and green colours

- begin to understand the concept of time – they remember events in the past and can anticipate events in the future

Copying a circle, using a dynamic tripod grip

- are fascinated by cause and effect and often ask 'Why?'

- can sort objects into simple categories

- remember and repeat songs and nursery rhymes

- understand the concept of 'one' and 'lots'

- count by rote up to ten, but do not appreciate quantity beyond two or three

- use personal pronouns and plurals correctly and can give their own name and sex, and sometimes age

- carry on simple conversations, often missing link words such as 'the' and 'is'

- learn to speak more than one language if they hear more than one language spoken around them as they grow

- still talk to themselves when playing

- enjoy listening to and making music

- can control their attention, choosing to stop an activity and return to it without much difficulty.

Emotional and social development

Children:

- like to do things unaided
- enjoy family mealtimes
- can think about things from someone else's point of view
- show affection for younger siblings
- manage to use the lavatory independently, and are often dry through the night (though this is variable between children, and from day to day with a given child)
- enjoy helping adults, as in tidying up
- are willing to share toys with other children and are beginning to take turns when playing
- often develop fears, for example of the dark, as they become capable of pretending and imagining
- are becoming aware of being male or female (are developing a gender role)
- make friends and are interested in having friends.

Moral and spiritual development

Children:

- are beginning to develop the concept of being helpful
- believe that all rules are fixed and unchallengeable – for example, if told that coats must be worn when playing outside, they accept this without question.

Play

Children:

- like to ride tricycles and play outdoors

- enjoy simple craft activities, for example with scissors and beads, and playing with dough

- join in active pretend play with other children

- enjoy playing on the floor with bricks, boxes, trains and dolls, both alone and with others

- like jigsaw puzzles and making models.

Promoting development

- Provide a wide variety of playthings – balls for throwing and catching, sand, jigsaw puzzles, and so on.

- Encourage play with other children.

- Provide a variety of art and craft activities: thick crayons, stubby paint brushes, paper, paint, and dough for modelling or play cooking.

- Talk to children often and read to them, to encourage the development of language.

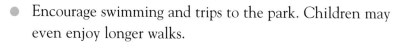

- Encourage swimming and trips to the park. Children may even enjoy longer walks.

Playing with other children

- Promote independence by teaching children how to look after and put away their own clothes and toys.

- Provide toys for water play, perhaps in the bath or paddling pool.

- Let them help you cook – you could make some biscuits.

- Encourage visits to the library and story times.

- Play simple matching and sorting games with them, such as lotto.

During cookery activities, never let the child use the oven or handle hot liquids. Make sure that any spills are wiped up promptly.

If cooking within a nursery setting, keep the maximum number of children to four.

Always supervise water play.

Activities

➤ *Making music using instruments*

You can help children to make a range of percussive (beating) and shaking instruments.

1 Collect together tins to beat with wooden spoons, saucepan lids to clash together, and securely closed jars containing pasta or pulses to shake.

2 Look for anything that children can safely manipulate and that makes an interesting sound.

➤ *Making music using the voice*

Making music together

The voice is the most natural musical instrument there is. As well as speaking and singing with it, you can make a whole range of different sounds. This activity encourages experimentation and, with the help of a tape-recorder, allows children to find out what they can do with their voice.

1 You need a portable tape-recorder with a built-in microphone.

2 If the child is not already familiar with it, demonstrate the workings of the tape-recorder.

3 You could start off with the child singing a favourite song or rhyme: then playing the tape back to hear how it sounds. You could talk about the different sounds on the tape, and begin to describe them.

4 Try the following ideas:

- Speak in a very high and very low voice.
- Speak very fast or very slowly.
- Whisper very quietly – close to the microphone.
- Shout – a long way from the microphone!
- Make animal noises.
- Hum a tune.

Ideas for students

1 Make a detailed observation of the activity.

2 Outline the possible benefits to the child, and write an evaluation.

➤ *Picture lotto*

You can buy a ready-made lotto game, but you might enjoy making your own.

1 Find some suitable illustrations for a simple picture lotto game.

2 Make your picture lotto game by pasting three sets of eight or more coloured pictures of toys or household objects onto three large pieces of card. Cut round the pictures on two of the cards, leaving one as your playing board.

3 To play lotto, simply fill up the playing board by turning over cards that match.

Games such as lotto encourage the concept of one-to-one correspondence, which is vital for the child's understanding of number.

Playing picture lotto

Ideas for students

If you have access to the Internet, you could collect some interesting pictures by visiting the BBC Education website, for example, to print pictures of Tweenies or other cartoon characters.

Chapter 11
Four years

At 4 years of age, children are quite capable and independent.

They walk with swinging steps, almost like an adult's, and like to hop and jump.

They are fascinated by cause and effect, and their increasing mastery of language prompts them to ask questions about the way things work in the world.

Physical development

Gross motor skills

Children:

- have developed a good sense of balance and may be able to walk along a line

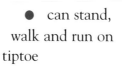

- can stand, walk and run on tiptoe

- can catch, kick, throw and bounce a ball

- bend at the waist to pick up objects from the floor

- enjoy climbing trees and on frames

- run up and down stairs, one foot per step

- can ride a tricycle with skill and make sharp turns easily.

Moving with a good sense of balance

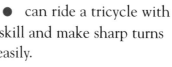

Walking down stairs as an adult would

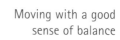

Running on tiptoe

Fine motor skills

Children:

- can build a tower of ten or more cubes

- can copy a building pattern of three steps using six cubes or more

- are able to thread small beads on a lace

- hold and use a pencil in adult fashion

- can draw on request a figure that resembles a person, showing head, legs and body

Copying a building pattern including bridges

- can copy the letters 'X', 'V', 'H', 'T' and 'O'

- can spread their hand, and can bring their thumbs into opposition with each finger in turn.

Copying circles and crosses

Sensory development

Children:

- match and name four primary colours

- listen to long stories with attention.

Cognitive and language development

Children:

- enjoy counting up to twenty by rote, and understand the concept of number up to three

- talk about things in the past and the future

- can sort objects into groups

- have increased memory skills – for example, they can remember a particular event, such as when their grandparents visited several months previously

- can give reasons and solve problems

- include more detail in their drawings, such as adding hands and fingers to drawings of people

- often confuse fact with fiction

- talk fluently, asking questions ('Why … ?', 'When … ?', 'How … ?') and understanding the answers

- can repeat nursery rhymes and songs, with very few errors

- can state their full name and address almost correctly

- tell long stories, sometimes confusing fact and fantasy

- enjoy jokes and plays on words

- may begin to recognise patterns in the way words are formed and apply these consistently, unaware that many common words have irregular forms – for example, as the past tense is often made by adding '-ed' ('I walk' becomes 'I walked'), children may say 'I runned' or 'I goed' instead of 'I ran' or 'I went'.

Sharing a picture book

Emotional and social development

Children:

- can eat skilfully with a spoon and a fork
- can wash and dry their hands, and brush their teeth
- can undress and dress themselves, except for laces, ties and back buttons
- often show sensitivity to others
- show a sense of humour, both in talk and in activities
- like to be independent and are strongly self-willed
- like to be with other children.

Dressing unaided

Moral and spiritual development

Children:

- understand the needs of others and the need to share and take turns
- try to work out what is 'right' and what is 'wrong' in behaviour.

The development of play

Children:

- act out puppet shows and scenes they have seen on television
- play elaborate role-play games with others
- enjoy imaginative play, which helps them to cope with strong emotions.

Promoting development

- Provide children with plenty of opportunities for exercise.
- Play party games such as musical statues, to foster the ideas of winning, losing, and co-operation.
- Encourage children to use rope swings and climbing frames.
- Encourage play with small construction toys, jigsaw puzzles and board games.
- Provide art and craft materials for painting, printing, and gluing and sticking activities.
- Encourage sand and water play, and play with dough or modelling clay.
- Talk often with children. Repeat favourite stories and encourage them to express themselves.
- Visit the library and read books together.
- Look for books and puzzles that help children to categorise and sort objects.
- Play lotto and other matching games such as pairs (pelmanism).
- Display children's paintings around the house – this gives them a feeling of pride in their work.
- Teach children how to dress and undress themselves in preparation for school games lessons.
- Encourage independence when going to the toilet.
- Let children practise using a computer mouse and carrying out simple computer activities.

- Organise visits to parks and farms. Encourage children to draw what they have seen.

- Involve children in caring for pets to encourage a sense of responsibility.

- Provide a box of dressing-up clothes for imaginative play.

- Let children organise their own games with friends, to encourage independence and confidence.

- Try not to rush to help when children are finding an activity difficult – allow them time to master new skills, offering praise and encouragement.

Safety points

Teach children never to play with sticks or other sharp objects, or to run with a pencil or lolly stick in their mouth.

Teach children not to eat berries or fungi.

Educate children about road safety by setting a good example.

Activities

➤ *Making a book*

Helping children to make a book of their own is a good way of encouraging a liking for books.

One idea is to make a book about the child and about the people and things that mean a lot to her or him. This could include drawings or photographs of:

- family and friends

- toys and favourite things

- birthdays and holidays

- pets and other animals

- favourite foods and games.

The book need not be elaborate; the main idea is to involve the child in the making of it and thereby increase her or his **self-esteem**. You could buy a scrapbook or a large notebook, or just fold some large sheets of paper in half, punch holes along the fold, and thread some ribbon or cord through them.

➤ *Growing mustard and cress*

Children will enjoy growing their own plants and discovering how to care for them.

1   Collect some empty eggshells. Give each child a shell and ask them to draw a face on their own shell.

2   Cut a cardboard egg carton into individual pockets. Place one eggshell in each pocket.

3   Pack each shell generously with cotton wool and soak this with water before putting the seeds on top.

4   Water the cotton wool regularly and wait for the 'green hair' to sprout. (This should only take two or three days.)

Chapter 12
Five years

Children enjoy showing what they can do – hopping, skipping, dancing and playing group ball games.

They have a growing awareness of the world, and their language shows this understanding.

Children are learning self-control, including how to wait, and how to take turns.

They are completely independent in everyday skills, such as washing, dressing and eating.

Physical development

Gross motor skills

Children:

- have increased agility – they can run and dodge, run lightly on their toes, climb and skip

- show good balance – they can stand on one foot for about ten seconds, and some may ride a bike without stabilisers

- show good co-ordination, playing ball games and dancing rhythmically to music

- can bend at the waist and touch their toes without bending at the knees

- can hop 2–3 m (6–9 feet) forwards on each foot separately

- use a variety of play equipment, including slides, swings and climbing frames.

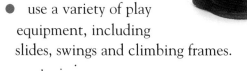

Bending at the waist and touching the toes

Fine motor skills

Children:

- can use a knife and fork competently, but may still need to have meat cut up for them

- may be able to thread a large-eyed needle and sew with large stitches

- have good control over pencils and paintbrushes

- can draw a person with a head, a body, legs, a nose, a mouth and eyes

- can copy elaborate models, such as a four-step model using ten cubes

Painting a person

- can construct elaborate models using kits (such as Duplo®)

- can copy a square and, at 5½ years, a triangle

- can copy letters 'V', 'T', 'H', 'O', 'X', 'L', 'A', 'C', 'U' and 'Y'

- can count the fingers on one hand using the index finger of the other

- can do jigsaw puzzles with interlocking pieces.

Sensory development

Children:

- can match ten or twelve colours.

Constructing an elaborate model

Cognitive and language development

Children:

- produce drawings with good detail – for example, a house with windows, a door, a roof and a chimney

- ask about abstract words (for instance, 'What does "beyond" mean?')

- can give their full name, age and address, and often their birthday

- are interested in reading and writing

- recognise their name and attempt to write it

- talk about the past, present and future, with a good sense of time

- are fluent in their speech and grammatically correct

- love to be read stories and will then act them out in detail later, either alone or with friends

- enjoy jokes and riddles.

Emotional and social development

Children:

- dress and undress alone, but may have difficulty with shoelaces
- have very definite likes and dislikes, some with little apparent logic – for example, a child might eat carrots when cut into strips but not when cut into rounds
- are able to amuse themselves for longer periods of time, looking at a book or watching a video
- show sympathy, and comfort friends who are hurt
- enjoy caring for pets
- choose their own friends.

Moral and spiritual development

Children:

- understand the social rules of their culture, for example the usual way to greet somebody
- instinctively help other children when they are distressed.

Play

Children:

- enjoy team games and games with rules
- may show a preference for a particular sport or craft activity
- play complicated games on the floor with miniature objects (**small-world play**)
- play alone or with others
- enjoy elaborate pretend play with others.

Playing with a younger child

Promoting development

- Provide plenty of outdoor activities.

- Provide stilts to encourage balance and co-ordination – these could be made from old paint cans and strong cord.

- Teach children to ride a two-wheeled bicycle.

- Teach children to swim.

- Encourage non-stereotypical activities, such as boys using skipping ropes and girls playing football.

- Team sports may be provided at school or at clubs such as Beavers, Rainbows and Woodcraft Folk.

- Encourage the use of models, jigsaws, sewing kits and craft activities, as well as drawing and painting.

- Talk to children about past, present and future, to promote language skills.

- Allow children to organise their own games.

- Encourage children to help with simple tasks, such as washing-up or watering plants.

- Set clear boundaries for behaviour, and always explain these to children.

Balancing on stilts

Safety points

If you have large picture windows, mark them with coloured strips to make it obvious when they are closed.

When out at dusk or when walking on country roads without pavements, use luminous armbands or light-coloured clothing for children.

Activities

➤ Conservation of number

Conservation is the name for the concept that objects remain the same in fundamental ways, such as in their volume or number, even when there are external changes in their shape or arrangement.

This activity uses buttons. The object of this activity is to see whether the child recognises that the same number of buttons remain, even when they have been arranged differently.

1 Make two rows of buttons. Check that the child agrees that the two rows contain the same number in each row.

2 Spread one row out to make a longer row. Ask the child which row contains *more* buttons.

Checking that the number of buttons is the same in each row

Ideas for students

Jean Piaget (1896–1980) was a psychologist who studied the way in which children developed intellectually. Piaget stated that children under 7 years old will not conserve when presented with the activity above. However, other researchers have found that children as young as 5 or 6 years old are able to understand that objects remain the same, even when arranged differently.

1 You could try this simple experiment with several children aged 5, 6 and 7 years old.

2 Summarise your findings.

➤ *Feeding the birds*

This activity encourages the development of caring for living things, knowledge and understanding of the natural world, and manual dexterity. It is particularly suitable for a winter's day.

First you could talk to the child about the birds in wintertime:

- Why will it be difficult for them to find food?
- How could you help them?

Then you could suggest that you make the birds some bird 'cakes'. You will need:

- mixed garden bird food (or you can mix your own from finely chopped nuts, millet, oatmeal, sunflower seed, chopped apple and dried fruit)
- empty yoghurt pots
- lengths of string
- lard or suet
- a mixing bowl
- a tray and a wooden spoon.

Making the bird cakes:

1 Encourage the child to mix all the dry ingredients in the bowl, using the wooden spoon.

2 Meantime, start to melt the lard or suet very carefully, well out of the child's reach.

3 Make a large chunky knot at one end of a piece of string. Coil that end at the base of the yoghurt pot, leaving a good tail coming out at the top of the pot.

4 Help the child to spoon the dry mixture into the pots all around the string. Leave about 2 cm (1 inch) at the top still to fill.

5 Place your filled pots on a tray and lift this out of the child's reach.

6 Carefully pour the melted fat around the mixture. Stir it in, and put the 'cakes' in a cool, safe place to set.

7 When set, remove the bird cake from the pots. Go with the child to tie them up. Hang them where you will have a good view from a window, and make sure that they are well out of the reach of cats.

Remember that when you start to feed birds, they come to depend on you as a food source. Having started, you need to continue to feed them throughout the winter.

You could use a bird book to identify your visitors, and a bird diary to remember their names.

Chapter 13
Six years

Children of 6 years are full of curiosity, and are developing their own interests.

They are forming new concepts of size, shape, weight and distance.

They are growing towards reading and writing independently, putting words and ideas down on paper, and often using invented spelling.

Physical development

Gross motor skills

Children:

- are gaining in both strength and agility: they can jump off apparatus at school with confidence

- can run and jump, and can kick a football up to 6m (9 feet) away

- can hop easily, with good balance

Jumping with confidence

- can catch and throw balls with accuracy

- can ride a two-wheeled bike, usually using stabilisers at first

- can skip in time to music, alternating their feet.

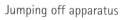

Jumping off apparatus

Hopping with good balance

Fine motor skills

Children:

- can build a tower of cubes that is virtually straight

- can hold a pencil in a hold similar to that of an adult (the dynamic tripod grip)

Using a pencil with a dynamic tripod grip

- are able to write a number of letters of similar size

- can write their last name as well as their first name

Writing a name

- may begin to write simple stories.

Building straight towers

Cognitive and language development

Children:

- begin to think in a more co-ordinated way, and can hold more than one point of view at a time

- begin to develop concepts of quantity: length, measurement, distance, area, time, volume, capacity and weight

- are able to distinguish the difference between reality and fantasy, but are often still frightened by supernatural characters in books, on the television, and so on

Exploring concepts of quantity

- are interested in basic scientific principles and are beginning to understand, for example, what happens to everyday materials if they are soaked or heated
- are increasingly influenced by cultural conventions in drawing and writing, for example often combining their own personal symbols with letters from the alphabet
- draw people in detail, including for instance eyebrows and eyelashes, and buttons and laces on clothes
- can pronounce the majority of the sounds of their own language
- talk fluently and with confidence
- can remember and repeat nursery rhymes and songs
- are steadily developing **literacy** skills (reading and writing), although the ability to read independently usually begins between 7 and 9 years of age
- alternate between wanting stories read to them and reading books themselves.

Emotional and social development

Children:

- can carry out simple tasks, such as peeling vegetables, watering plants, hanging up clothes and tidying the contents of drawers
- choose friends mainly because of their personality and interests
- can hold a long conversation with another child or an adult, naturally taking turns in speaking and listening
- begin to compare themselves with other people – 'I am like her in that way, but different in this way …'.

Moral and spiritual development

Children:

- are beginning to develop further concepts, such as being forgiving, and fairness.

Play

Children:

- play together with other children (**co-operative play**)
- assign roles to others in elaborate pretend play and role-play
- role-play situations of which they have no direct experience but which might happen to them one day, such as getting married, or travelling through space to the moon (**fantasy play**).

Promoting development

- Provide opportunity for vigorous exercise.
- Allow children to try a new activity or sport, such as football, dancing, judo or gymnastics.
- Encourage writing skills by providing lots of examples of things written for different purposes, such as shopping lists, letters and recipes.
- Play memory games with children, such as pairs and dominoes.
- Talk to children about what they have done during the day.
- Encourage children to sort and match objects. Ask them to order things according to more abstract concepts, such as sweetness or preference.
- Try not to correct grammatical mistakes – instead, respond by subtly rephrasing their statement while showing that you have understood them. Thus a child might say, 'A lion is more fiercer than a cat', and you could reply, 'Yes, lions *are* fiercer than cats'.
- Create a warm supporting atmosphere during story time at home or at school, with plenty of talk about the story you are reading.

Safety points

Give children clear guidelines about safety. For example:

- never climb a tree without first asking an adult's permission
- never cross a road without an accompanying adult
- never accept anything offered by a stranger
- never, ever, go anywhere with a stranger.

Activities

➤ *Cooking biscuits*

Making biscuits gives plenty of opportunities for measuring, mixing, rolling out, cutting shapes and decorating.

Get together everything you will need before you begin, so that you do not have to leave children unsupervised. If cooking at school, limit the number of children to four. Follow these guidelines:

Making biscuits

- Teach children to wash their hands and dry them thoroughly before cooking.

- Teach them to be very careful when handling knives.

- Teach them to ask before tasting anything.

- Clear up any spills immediately.

Here is a basic biscuit recipe:

- 125 g (4 oz) soft margarine or butter
- 125 g (4 oz) sugar (white or brown)
- 250 g (8 oz) plain flour
- 1 egg
- pinch of salt
- (grated orange or lemon rind if desired).

Making the biscuits:

1 Pre-heat the oven (moderate: 190 °C, 375 °F or gas mark 5).
2 Beat the margarine and sugar together.
3 Beat the egg and add to the mixture.
4 Sift in the flour and the salt (and the grated rind, if used).
5 Mix to form a ball of dough.
6 Roll out the dough to a thickness of 0.5 cm ($^1/_4$ inch). Cut into shapes.
7 Put the shapes on a greased baking tray, and bake them in the middle of the oven for about 15 minutes.

Ideas for students

Make a detailed observation of the activity. Notice the language used by the children, and the understanding of concepts that they demonstrate.

➤ *Early science*

Try out this simple demonstration of static electricity with a child or a group of children.

1 Stir a little salt and pepper together.
2 Ask the child to separate them using a teaspoon. This, of course, is not possible.
3 Then rub the spoon against a sweater – ideally one made of acrylic or another synthetic fibre. This creates static electricity on the spoon.
4 Simply hold the spoon just above the mixture. Pepper is lighter than salt, and the static electricity on the spoon will lift it free from the salt.

Chapter 14
Seven years

Children at 7 have a well-developed sense of balance and enjoy activities that involve precise movements, such as hopscotch or skipping games.

They are interested in talking, listening, and reading and writing, and enjoy games with rules.

They have a clear sense of right and wrong, and see friendships as very important.

Physical development

Gross motor skills

Walking along a narrow wall

Children:

● can hop on either leg, and can walk along a thin line with their arms outstretched for balance

● may be expert at riding a two-wheeled bike or using roller skates

● can climb on play apparatus with skill, some managing to climb ropes

● have increased stamina, shown in activities such as swimming, skating, gymnastics and martial arts

● are able to control their speed when running and can swerve to avoid collision

● are skilful in catching and throwing a ball, using one hand only.

Catching a ball with one hand

Climbing skilfully on play apparatus

Fine motor skills

Children:

- can build tall, straight towers with cubes

- are more competent in their writing skills – individual letters are more clearly differentiated now, and capital and small letters are in proportion

- begin to use colour in a naturalistic way, for example using a band of green colour at the bottom of the page to represent grass, and a band of blue across the top to represent sky

- draw people with heads, bodies, hands, hair, fingers and clothes

- can use a large needle to sew with thread.

Drawing a person in detail

Cognitive and language development

Children:

- are able to conserve number – for example, they know that there are ten sweets whether they are pushed close together or spread apart

- express themselves in speech and writing

- can use a computer mouse and keyboard for simple word-processing

- enjoy the challenge of experimenting with new materials, and enjoy learning mathematical and scientific concepts, such as adding and subtracting numbers

- perform simple calculations in their head

- begin to understand how to tell the time

Using a computer mouse and keyboard

- may be interested in design and in working models
- enjoy learning about living things and about the world around them
- are able to arrive at logical conclusions and to understand cause and effect.

Emotional and social development

Children:

- learn how to control their emotions – they realise that they can keep their own thoughts private and hide their true feelings
- begin to think in terms not only of who they are, but also of who they would *like* to be
- are completely independent in washing, dressing and toileting skills
- may be able to speak up for themselves, for example when visiting the dentist or the doctor
- may be critical of their own work at school
- form friendships which are very important to them
- form close friends, mostly within their own sex.

Moral and spiritual development

Children:

- have a clear sense of right and wrong – for example, they realise that it is wrong to hurt other people physically
- express feelings of awe and wonder, particularly about nature, plants and insects.

Play

Children:

- engage in complex co-operative play, using more people, props and ideas
- take part in games with rules.

Promoting development

- Encourage vigorous outdoor play – on swings and climbing frames, and in skipping and hopping games such as hopscotch.

- Take children swimming, skating or riding, or to a dancing or martial arts class.

- Arrange an obstacle course for children to navigate bikes around.

- Provide a range of drawing and craft materials, such as charcoal, paint, clay and materials for collage.

- Help children to make a safe 'den', using a tepee design with sticks and a blanket.

- Encourage children in simple gardening skills, such as digging, planting, raking and watering.

- Promote creative expression in the form of written stories, poetry, dance, drama and making music.

- Take children to see plays and puppet shows.

- Involve children in a puppet show – both in making the puppets and in acting out a play.

- Try some simple cause-and-effect experiments. For example, you could demonstrate how a waterwheel works.

- Try growing some simple crystals.

- Encourage children to plan and make working models, such as cranes, pulley lifts and wheeled vehicles, using recycled materials.

- Introduce children to the customs of different religions, such as Diwali, Ramadan, and Christmas.

- Encourage children to become more familiar with using a computer, for instance keying in letters, numbers and punctuation marks.

- Encourage children to share stories together – even a child who is not yet fluent at reading will still enjoy being able to read to a younger child.

- Allow children to run simple errands on their own, for example to post a letter.

Safety points

Teach children never to put a plastic bag on their head.

Teach children only ever to buy sweets from a shop, and never to accept them from a stranger.

Activities

➤ *Number bonds*

This is a game that can be played by two people. One player calls out a number under ten. The other player answers with the number that brings the *total* of the two numbers to ten.

This has to be done as quickly as possibly. If you hesitate, you are out! For example:

> Player 1, 'Six'; Player 2, 'Four'.
> Player 1, 'Two'; Player 2, 'Eight'.
> Player 1, 'Three'; Player 2, 'Er … er …!'

Player 2 is out! Take it in turns to go first. Before you start, decide how many times you are going to play the game.

When the child is confident about numbers adding up to ten, you can vary the game by moving up to a larger number. Try twenty. Then go on to one hundred. Children may need a little more time to think as the numbers get bigger.

➤ *A sound experiment*

Make a yogurt pot telephone.

You will need:

- two empty, clean yoghurt pots
- a ball of string
- scissors.

To make the telephone:

1   Using the scissors, make a small hole in the bottom of each of the pots.

2   Cut a very long piece of string, and push one end through the bottom of each pot.

3   Tie a knot inside each pot to stop the string from coming out.

4   Ask a child to hold one of the pots to his or her ear. Now move away from the child until the string is straight and pulled tight. (You could do this yourself, or give the second pot to another child.)

5   Now send a telephone message to the child by speaking into the pot.

Children will learn that the sound of a voice makes the pot vibrate, and that the vibrations pass as sound waves along the string to the other pot, and into the other person's ear.

Chapter 15
Developmental assessment

This section looks briefly at the standard developmental assessments carried out on children from birth to the age of 5. After the age of 5 years, the school health service takes over the assessments.

If a child has a developmental delay, carers will want to know about the problem as soon as possible: it is easier to come to terms with a serious problem in a young baby than in an older child.

Health professionals should always take carers' concerns seriously and must never treat parents or other carers as fussy, neurotic or over-anxious.

Parent-held records

In most clinics carers are given a personal child health record or a record to keep for their baby. This is a way of keeping track of the child's progress.

Records are kept of the child's:

- height and weight
- immunisations
- childhood illnesses and accidents.

Development reviews

Regular development reviews are carried out in child health clinics and at the child's home by general practitioners, health visitors and school nurses. If the child's first language is not English, development reviews can be carried out with the help of someone who can speak the child's language.

Children's holistic development is reviewed:

- gross motor skills: sitting, standing, walking, running
- fine motor skills: handling toys, stacking bricks, doing up buttons and tying shoelaces (gross and fine manipulative skills)
- speech and language, including hearing
- vision
- social behaviour.

Reviews give carers opportunities to say what they have noticed about their child. They can also discuss anything that concerns them about their child's health and behaviour.

Ages for reviews

Note that in some parts of the country, especially after the age of 3, the ages at which children are reviewed may vary slightly from those given below.

Assessment of the newborn baby

Shortly after birth, the newborn baby is examined by the **paediatrician** or family doctor. Specific checks are made to assess the development of the baby:

- the baby is weighed

- the spine is checked for any evidence of **spina bifida**

- the mouth is checked for evidence of a **cleft palate** – a gap in the roof of the mouth

- the head is checked for size and shape, and the head circumference is measured

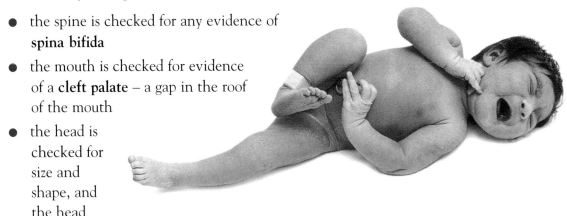

A newborn baby

- the eyes are checked for **cataract**

- the neck is examined for any obvious injury to the neck muscles after a difficult birth

- the hands are checked for webbing (fingers joined together at the base) or creases (a single unbroken crease from one side of the palm to the other is one feature of **Down's syndrome**)

- the hips are tested for congenital dislocation

- the feet are checked for webbing and **talipes** (club foot)

- the reflex actions are observed (see pages 8 and 9)

- the hearing is tested, often by means of **Otoacoustic Emissions Testing (OAE)** or the 'cradle test': this involves placing a sponge earphone into the ear canal, then stimulating the ear with sound and measuring an 'echo' – the echo is found in all normal-hearing individuals, so its absence may indicate a hearing loss and the need for further testing.

Other medical checks include:

- listening to the heart and lungs to detect any abnormality

- examining the anus and the genitalia for any malformation.

Assessment at 6–8 weeks

Developmental reviews from 6 weeks onwards are conducted under these headings: 'Discussion', 'Observation', 'Measurement' and 'Examination'.

Discussion

Carers are asked if they have any general concerns about their baby, in particular about:

- feeding
- sleeping
- bowel actions and passing urine.

They are also asked whether they think that the baby can:

- hear – for example, does the baby 'startle' to a sudden noise?
- see – for example, does the baby turn her or his head to follow the carer?

Observation

While the carer is undressing the baby for examination, the doctor will look out for:

- the responsiveness of the baby – smiles, eye contact, attentiveness to the carer's voice, and so on
- any difficulties the carer has in holding the baby – for example, a depressed mother will lack visual attention and may not hold and support the baby adequately
- any signs of jaundice or anaemia.

This is also an opportunity to provide help and support to the baby's main carers.

Measurement

The baby is weighed naked and the weight plotted on a **growth (centile) chart**.

The head circumference is measured and plotted on the growth chart.

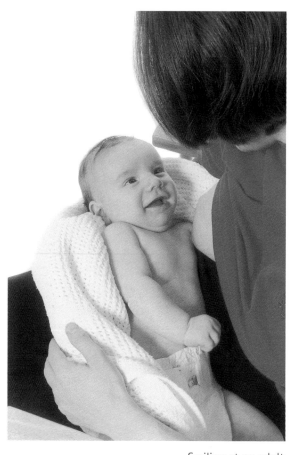

Smiling at an adult

Examination

The general appearance of the baby will indicate general health and whether he or she is well nourished.

In addition:

- The eyes are inspected using a light – babies will turn their head and follow a small light beam.
- The heart and hips are checked again.
- The baby is placed in the prone position, in which he or she will turn the head to one side, and hold the hands with the thumbs inwards and the fingers wrapped around them.
- The **posterior fontanelle** is usually closed by now; the **anterior fontanelle** does not close until around 18 months.

Assessment at 6–9 months

Discussion

Carers are asked whether they have any concerns about their baby's health and development.

Observation

The doctor will note:

- socialisation and **attachment** behaviour, particularly how the baby interacts with the carer – most babies are clingy at this age
- **communication** – sounds, expression and gestures
- **motor development** – sitting, balance, use of hands, any abnormal movement patterns.

While the baby is sitting on the carer's lap, the doctor will also observe the baby's muscle tone.

Measurement

The baby's head circumference and weight are measured and plotted on the growth chart.

The assessment checks that both hands are used equally

Specialist help

Many services are available to help children who have special needs to learn and develop. For example:

- *physiotherapy*
- *speech and language therapy*

A group of children in a children's centre

- *occupational therapy*
- *home learning schemes* – for example, the Portage scheme provides trained home visitors to work with parents and their young children
- the provision of *equipment and special aids* such as pushchairs, wheelchairs, communication aids, or hearing aids
- *financial support* to help families where children need help with personal care and/or mobility

- *toy libraries* – most areas have a toy library for children with special needs from which specially chosen toys can be borrowed for use at home
- *specialist playgroups*, *opportunity groups* and *children's centres* – these centres often provide on-site physiotherapy, nursing care and play therapy
- *respite care* – for instance, Crossroads is a national voluntary organisation that provides trained care assistants for the practical respite care needed by some children with disabilities
- *playgroups* – state-run, privately run, or voluntary
- *nurseries*, *school nurseries* and *classes*.

To find out what's available in your area, ask your health visitor, your GP, the social services department, or the educational adviser for special needs at your local education department.

Promoting development in children with special needs

Many children with special needs who attend mainstream nurseries and schools will require one-to-one attention from a trained early years worker. The following section provides some ideas for those working with children with special needs.

Children with physical impairments

Children with physical limitations have specific needs depending on their particular disability.

Friends and classmates are usually eager to assist a child with a physical difficulty. Although such helpful behaviour should be applauded, children with physical problems also need encouragement to do as much as possible for themselves. This may mean that tasks and chores take a little more time, but being patient and encouraging promotes self-confidence and independence.

Difficulties

Children who have difficulties with gross motor skills:

- may stumble and trip frequently
- may have difficulty walking or running, jumping or climbing, or be unable to do these at all
- may have poor balance
- may have difficulty in bouncing, catching, or throwing balls
- may be unable to release objects voluntarily.

Children who have difficulties with fine motor skills:

- may have poorly developed hand or finger co-ordination
- may have difficulty in picking up small objects
- may have difficulty in drawing or writing.

Throwing bean bags promotes physical development and coordination skills

Promoting development

Make sure that the environment is suitable:

- Check that doors are wide enough, that door handles can be reached and that toileting facilities are accessible.
- Provide heavy, stable furniture and equipment that are not easily knocked over.
- Avoid area rugs. Arrange furniture and equipment to allow for a wide pathway for users of walking frames or wheelchairs.
- Provide a safe place to store walkers, crutches, sticks or canes so that other children do not trip over them.

Provide suitable equipment:

- Provide objects that can be used for grasping, holding, transferring and releasing. Make sure that the object is appropriate for the child's age – for instance, a bean bag made from dinosaur fabric is much more appropriate for a 5-year-old than a rattle or baby toy.

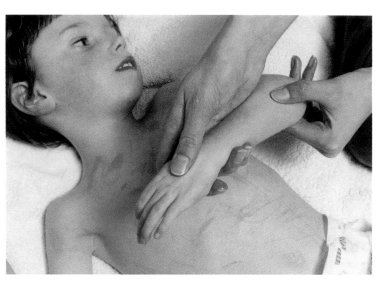

Using massage promotes muscle relaxation and enjoyment

- Work with parents and carers to find comfortable ways for children to sit. For example, one child may like a corner with two walls for support, another may need a chair with a seat belt, or a wheelchair with a large tray across the arms.
- Make objects as steady as possible. For instance, fix paper, mixing bowls or wood blocks to the table or floor with tape so that they remain secure when the child is painting, drawing, stirring or hammering.

- Provide materials of different textures – such as play dough, fabric swatches, ribbon, corrugated cardboard, and sandpaper – to encourage the sense of touch.

Offer appropriate activities:

- Plan activities to encourage exercise and movement of all body parts.
- Work with parents or carers and specialists to give special exercises for children, depending on each child's individual needs.

Children with visual impairment

Most children who are considered visually impaired do have *some* usable vision. Even those considered blind are often able to tell the difference between light and dark.

Children with visual impairment are frequently delayed in their physical and motor skills; for example, they may not be able to locate or pick up small objects they have dropped. Helping children understand about space and size will help to promote their development.

Difficulties

Children:

- may sometimes or always cross one or both eyes
- may have eyes that won't focus
- may blink or rub their eyes a lot
- may tilt their head to the side or the front
- may squint or frown a great deal
- may be unable to locate and pick up small objects that have been dropped
- may turn their face away when being addressed, if they are using some peripheral vision
- may hold books or objects very close to their face
- may avoid bright lights
- may stumble or fall a great deal, or trip over small objects
- may cover one eye
- may appear inattentive
- may complain of dizziness, a headache or nausea after doing intense work.

Promoting development

Make sure that the environment is suitable:

- Provide cues – during dressing, eating, or any other daily activity, communicate clearly so that the child knows what will be happening.
- Avoid sudden changes of lighting. For example, when a child is to move from a darker hallway to a bright playroom, you could partially close the blinds before the child enters the playroom, and open them again after a few minutes when the eyes have had time to adjust.
- Keep cupboard doors fully open or fully closed. Pad table corners. Make sure there are no curled-up edges on rugs.

- Always keep furniture in the same place, so that the child can use it as a guide around the room.
- Keep toys, personal items and the potty-chair within easy reach.

Provide suitable equipment:

- Offer babies objects for play that have hard, shiny surfaces – visually impaired babies often find furry objects off-putting.

Using a moving toy to promote the development of reach and of visual tracking

- Using an adult-sized toilet may make a young child with a visual impairment feel insecure. A small potty-chair might be more comfortable because the child can feel the floor underfoot and get on and off the potty-chair without help.

- Use carefully chosen clues – sounds, textures, scents or highly visible objects – to help children move around the nursery more confidently. For example, you could have wind chimes on one door, and different floor textures in different areas.

Using a mirror and lights to promote visual co-ordination

- Look for toys and books with raised numerals, letters or designs that children can touch and explore.
- Cut out symbols, shapes, letters, and numbers from sandpaper or cardboard. Guide the child's hand over these shapes as you discuss them.

Offer appropriate activities:

- Take babies around the house and name the sound clues they hear, such as a ticking clock or a wind chime.
- Don't be too quick to 'rescue' children. Try to give them the *least* assistance possible. Rather than rush to their aid, always ask children if they need help.
- Ask carers whether their child likes to be touched. Some children with visual impairments don't, but most do. A simple touch on the shoulder can be very reassuring.
- Use language full of descriptions. Tell children about colours, the weather, and things that are happening around them. This may seem awkward at first, but you will get used to it.
- Use names. A child with a visual impairment may not be able to see the facial expressions or body language that show others which person is being spoken to, such as which child you have turned your head toward. Speak to each child by name, especially when there are other people in the room.
- Use your voice to communicate feelings and meaning. Tone and volume can communicate sadness, happiness, anger, or other emotions.
- Relate directions to body parts. Rather than say 'You dropped your mitten on the floor' say instead, 'You dropped your mitten on the floor in front of your right foot'.
- Tell children when you are leaving them. Encourage other children to do the same: they will learn quickly by example.
- Provide activities with sensory experiences. Children with visual impairment learn through hearing and touch. Sand and water play, collages, play dough, and finger-painting are good learning activities.
- Follow up descriptions with concrete experiences. For example, after reading the story of 'The Three Little Pigs', the child might find it interesting to feel the difference between straw, sticks, and bricks.
- Teach non-disabled children to identify themselves to children with visual disabilities, and to describe their art activities or building constructions in words.
- Encourage children to build *horizontally* with blocks. Children can feel shapes and lay blocks end to end or in different patterns without the frustration of falling blocks.

Children with hearing impairment

Children who have difficulty hearing need opportunities to learn how to listen and speak. Provide activities that encourage communication and language development. Children can develop important language skills with practice. Activities with very little verbal interaction are also very important.

Difficulties

Children:

- may not respond when spoken to
- may not startle at loud noise
- may not wake up in response to sound
- may talk, but be impossible to understand
- may leave out many sounds when talking
- may seem unable to follow verbal directions
- may hold their head so that one ear is turned toward the speaker
- may talk in a very loud or a very soft voice
- may coo or gurgle, but may not progress to saying words
- may not talk very much or not at all
- may talk in a monotone voice
- may interrupt conversations, or seem unaware that others are talking
- may be alert and attentive to things that can be seen, but not to those others would hear.

Puppet play promotes emotional and social development

Promoting development

Make sure that the environment is suitable:

- During activities, cut down on background noise from the radio and machines such as dishwashers. Use carpets, rugs and pillows to absorb excess sound.

- Provide children with visual cues. For example, label shelves with a picture of toys to make tidying away toys easier. Use pictures to illustrate the steps of a recipe during cooking activities.

- Make eye contact before you start to speak. A gentle tap on the shoulder will usually get a child's attention.

- Talk in a normal voice – do not shout. Use gestures and facial expressions to clarify your message.

Provide suitable equipment:

- Provide headphones, or set up a special area where a tape recorder can be played at a higher volume.

- Provide toys that make a lot of noise; children can feel the vibrations even when they cannot hear the sound.

- Find out how to look after hearing aids and how to protect them from loss or damage within the school or nursery – for example, sand and dirt can damage hearing aids.

Offer appropriate activities:

- Teach children to use gestures and sign language, for example **Signalong**, **Makaton** or **British Sign Language (BSL)**.

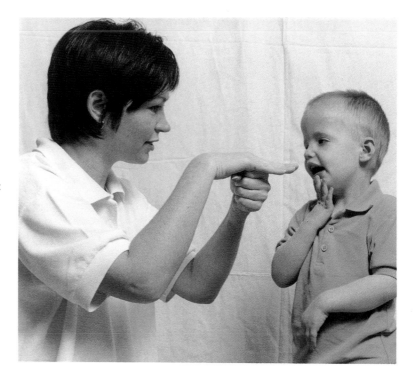

Using sign language (this is the Signalong symbol for 'more')

- Encourage children to talk about what they are doing. Ask open-ended questions that require an answer: these will encourage the child to practise using language.
- Use stories, songs, and finger-play to enhance language development.
- Repeat favourite rhymes and songs to encourage confidence in developing language skills.
- Encourage dancing to music; children will feel the vibrations and enjoy the chance to express themselves.

Children with learning disabilities

Children with learning disabilities will usually go through the typical sequence of developmental stages but at a much slower rate. Characteristics vary widely with different disabilities, but a few approaches can be applied to all kinds of disabilities.

Difficulties

Children:
- may have a short attention span and be easily distracted
- may have difficulty in making transitions, such as from one class to the next
- may prefer to play with younger children
- may speak and use language like a much younger child
- may be afraid of trying new things
- may have difficulty in problem-solving
- may not remember things well
- may not be able to transfer learning to a new situation
- may repeat the same movement over and over again.

A soft playroom provides a safe area for physical exercise and play

Promoting development

Make sure that the environment is suitable:

- Keep verbal instructions simple.
- Tell children how to do something and show them by guiding their hands and body through the movements of an activity.
- Avoid sudden transitions. When it's time to end an activity or to move to another activity, give the child plenty of warning.
- Provide cues to help children know what is expected from them – for example, mark their coat hook with a picture of a child hanging a coat up.
- Expect appropriate behaviour – don't allow a child with a learning disability to behave in ways that are not allowed in other children.
- Provide opportunities to play near a child who is doing a similar activity. This can give the child with learning difficulties some ideas on how to use and explore the same materials.

Playing alongside another child promotes social development

Offer appropriate activities:

- Break activities into small steps and give one instruction at a time.
- Practise activities over and over again.
- Allow children plenty of time to practise new things that they are learning.
- Select activities that match the child's mental age and abilities.
- Try not to overwhelm the child with too many toys or art materials at once.

Provide suitable equipment:

- Make sure that there are obvious differences in size, shape, and colour when sorting or classifying objects. Differences that are too subtle, such as between maroon and red, or oval shapes and circles, may be confusing.

Children with behavioural difficulties

Children with behavioural difficulties often display one of three types of extreme behaviour: withdrawal, aggression, or hyperactivity. Each type of behaviour may require a different strategy to promote social and emotional development.

Difficulties

Children:

- may use aggressive behaviour to deal with most situations
- may show extreme fear and anxiety
- may seem not to recognise basic feelings of happiness, sadness, anger, or fear
- may always react in the same way, such as crying or hitting
- may not want to be touched
- may withdraw or stay quiet and passive most of the time
- may show excessive activity, restlessness, or inability to stick to a task
- may regress to babyish behaviour whenever stress occurs
- may cry a great deal, seem depressed and unhappy, and seldom laugh.

Caring for pets promotes self-confidence and independence

Promoting development

Make sure that the environment is suitable:

- Treat children uniquely. Always take them seriously, and show that you believe in them.

- Listen to each child with respect. Don't compare the child who is being aggressive with another child who is playing well.

- Invite a withdrawn child to join in an activity by watching others. As the child becomes more comfortable, demonstrate how to play with materials or toys. Encourage the child to play along with you.

- Watch for signs of aggressive behaviour and intervene quickly. Teach problem-solving skills.

Offer appropriate activities:

- Provide developmentally appropriate activities which are not overly difficult and which will help the child feel capable. Avoid activities that can be done in only one way.

- Watch for periods when children are less excitable and more in control. Use these times to present a new activity that requires some concentration.

- Keep stories and group activities short to match attention spans. Seat the child near you and away from distractions such as a nearby shelf of toys.

- Avoid over-stimulation. Limit the number of toys or materials you set out at one time.

- Provide adult guidance and structure. Help children to plan or to organise an activity. For example, if a child wants to play at being a firefighter you could suggest some props, such as a bucket and a blanket, and perhaps invite other children to play.

- Announce the tidying-up time and other transitions ahead of time. During the transition, give the child a specific task.

Special needs assessment

Local education authorities who think that children over 2 years old may have special educational needs must make an assessment of their needs. For children under 2, an assessment must be made if parents ask for it.

This assessment is a way of getting advice about the child's educational needs, and parents can take part in the assessment. The Advisory Centre for Education (page 136) offers advice on education and produces a handbook on the subject.

Voluntary organisations

There are many voluntary organisations that focus on particular disabilities and illnesses; these organisations are a valuable source of information, advice and support for parents and professionals. Through them, parents can often be put in touch with other parents in similar situations. Contact a Family (page 136) is the national voluntary organisation that provides mutual support and advice for groups of families living in the same neighbourhood whose children have special needs.

Feeling part of a special group

Children with special needs – a checklist

The following questions can help parents and carers to ensure that they receive the help and support that they need.

- Is there a name for my child's condition? If so, what is it?
- Are more tests needed to get a clear diagnosis or to confirm what has been found out?
- Is the condition likely to get worse, or will it stay roughly the same?
- Where is the best place to go for medical help?
- Where is the best place to go for practical help?
- How can I get in touch with other parents who have children with a similar condition?
- How can I find out how best to help my child?

Glossary

anterior fontanelle A diamond-shaped soft area at the front of the head, just above the brow. It is a temporary gap between the bones of the head, and is covered by a tough membrane – often you can see the baby's pulse beating beneath the skin. The fontanelle closes between 12 and 18 months of age, when the bones fuse together.

articulation A person's actual pronunciation of words.

attachment An enduring emotional bond that an infant forms with a specific person. Usually the first attachment is to the mother, some time between the ages of 6 and 9 months.

attention deficit disorder (ADD) A behavioural disorder characterised by an inability to concentrate on tasks. In **attention deficit hyperactivity disorder (ADHD)**, inability to concentrate is accompanied or replaced by hyperactive and impulsive behaviour.

autism (autistic spectrum disorder) A rare developmental disorder which impairs a child's understanding of, and her or his ability to relate to, the environment.

bonding A term used to denote the feelings of love and responsibility that parents have for their babies.

British Sign Language (BSL) One of the languages used by those with a hearing impairment. To conduct a conversation, language users make **gestures** involving movements of their hands, arms, eyes, face and body.

casting Repeatedly throwing objects to the floor, in play or rejection.

cataract The loss of transparency of the crystalline lens of the eye.

central nervous system (CNS) The brain and the spinal cord, which are the main control centres of the body.

cerebral palsy A general term for disorders of movement and posture resulting from damage to the child's developing brain.

cleft palate A hole or split in the palate (the roof of the mouth).

coeliac disease A condition in which the lining of the small intestine is damaged by gluten, a protein found in wheat and rye.

cognitive (intellectual) Related to the ideas and thinking of the child. Cognition emphasises that children are aware, active learners, and that understanding is an important part of intellectual life.

comfort object (transitional object) An object, such as a blanket, a piece of cloth or a teddy, to which a child becomes especially attached.

communication Facial expression, body language, gestures, and verbal or sign language; talking about feelings, ideas and relationships using signs or words. (Language involves both **reception** – understanding – and **expression**.)

concept An overall idea formed in the mind which is based on and links past, present and future ideas that share some attributes. Thus a child may sit on a variety of actual chairs, but the *concept* of 'a chair' is an idea that develops in the child's mind.

conservation The concept that objects remain the same in basic ways, such as their weight or number, even when there are external changes in their shape or arrangement.

co-operative play Play in which children take account of other children's actions or roles within their play together – for instance, one might be the baby, the other the nurse, and the nurse might give medical treatment to the baby.

cradle test *See* **Otoacoustic Emissions Testing**.

creative play *See* **imaginative play**.

creativity The ability to make something from an idea one has imagined, for example a dance, a model, a poem or a mathematical equation: the process of creating something.

Down's syndrome A genetic anomaly which results in children having learning difficulties and characteristic physical features.

dynamic tripod grip Using the thumb and two fingers in a grip closely resembling the adult grip of a pencil or pen. *Compare* **primitive tripod grasp.**

dyslexia A specific reading disability, characterised by difficulty in coping with written symbols.

dyspraxia An immaturity of the brain such that some messages are not transmitted to the body. Children with dyspraxia often show behavioural difficulties and may be hyperactive.

echolalia The tendency of a child to echo the last words spoken by an adult.

empathy Awareness of another person's emotional state, and the ability to share the experience with that person.

evaluate To find out or judge the value of something.

expression Communication of what one thinks, feels or means, by word, facial expression, gesture or sign language.

expressive speech The words a person produces.

extension Stretching out.

fantasy play Play in which children role-play situations they do not fully know about but which might happen to them one day, such as going to hospital, or travelling to the moon in a space rocket.

fine manipulative skills Skills involving precise use of the hands and fingers in pointing, drawing, using a knife and fork, using chopsticks, writing, doing up shoelaces, and the like.

fine motor skills Skills including **gross manipulative skills**, which involve single limb movements, and **fine manipulative skills**, which involve precise movements of the hands and fingers.

flexion Bending.

gesture Any movement intended to convey meaning.

giftedness Having unusually great ability over a wide range of skills.

gross manipulative skills Skills involving single limb movements, usually of the arm, for example in throwing, catching and sweeping arm movements.

gross motor skills Skills involving the use of the large muscles in the body: they include walking, running, climbing, and the like.

growth (centile) chart A graph or chart used to plot the growth measurements (height and weight) of babies and children.

holistic Tending to see something in the round, for example seeing a child as a whole person, emotionally, intellectually, socially, physically, morally, culturally and spiritually.

holophrase The expression of a whole idea in a single word: thus 'car' may mean 'Give me the car' or 'Look at the car'.

imagination The ability to form new ideas which, though they may emerge from first-hand experiences of life, go beyond what one has experienced.

imaginative play (creative play) Play in which children draw on their own real-life experiences and rearrange them – for instance, they might make a pretend swimming pool from wooden blocks and then play out a rescue scene in which a child is saved from drowning in the pool by a lifeguard.

inclusive care and education The integration of disabled children into mainstream settings such as nursery schools, day nurseries, schools and family centres.

intellectual *See* **cognitive**.

labile Having rapidly fluctuating moods, such as cheerful one moment and angry the next.

literacy The ability to read and write: writing involves putting spoken language into a written code; reading involves decoding the written code into language.

Makaton A method of sign language that uses a combination of manual signs, graphic symbols and speech (the Makaton Vocabulary) to support spoken English.

meningitis Inflammation of the meninges in the lining of the brain.

motor development Growth and change in the ability to carry out physical activities, such as walking, running or riding a bicycle.

norm An average or typical state or ability, used with others as a framework for assessing development. Norms are the result of observations by many professionals in the field of child development.

normative Relating to norms or averages.

object permanence The recognition that an object continues to exist even when temporarily out of sight.

observation The process of watching accurately and taking notice.

Otoacoustic Emissions Testing (OAE, or cradle test) A hearing test. It is often called the 'cradle test' because it is performed on newborn babies.

paediatrician A qualified doctor who specialises in treating children.

palmar grasp Using the whole hand to grasp an object.

parallel play Play in which one child plays *alongside* another child, but not interacting with the other child.

perception The process by which events and information in the environment are transformed into an *experience* of objects, sounds, events, and the like.

personality The total combination of mental and behavioural characteristics that make each individual recognisably unique. Personality is affected by children's experiences of life and other people, as well as by the child's natural temperament.

pincer grip Using the thumb and fingers to grasp an object.

posterior fontanelle A small triangular-shaped soft area near the crown of the head. It is a temporary gap between the bones of the head, and is much smaller and less noticeable than the **anterior**

fontanelle. It usually closes by 6 to 8 weeks of age.

pretend play Play in which an action or object is given a symbolic meaning other than that from real life, such as when a clothes peg is used to represent a door key, or a large box to represent a boat.

primitive reflexes Automatic reactions to particular changes in surroundings – present in the newborn baby, and thought to be vital for the infant's survival. Reflexes give an indication of the baby's general condition and the normal functioning of the **central nervous system**. *See also* **reflex**.

primitive tripod grasp Grasping objects by use of the thumb and two fingers. *Compare* **dynamic tripod grip**.

prone Lying on one's face, or front downwards. *Compare* **supine.**

proprioception The sense that tells infants where the mobile parts of their body (such as their legs) are in relation to the rest of them.

reception (of language) Listening or watching and understanding language.

receptive speech The words a person understands.

reflex An automatic response to a stimulus. *See also* **primitive reflexes**.

role-play Play in which 'pretend' symbols are used together with activity – for example, a child pretends that a box is a car and then 'drives' to the shops.

self-concept How a child sees himself or herself; how the child believes others see him or her.

self-esteem The way a child feels about herself or himself: good feelings lead to high self-esteem, bad feelings lead to low self-esteem.

sensation Being aware of having an experience, through seeing, smelling, hearing, touching, tasting, or moving (kinaesthesia).

Signalong A method of signing (using gestures and symbols), used with children who have communication difficulties.

small-world play Play which involves the use of miniature objects, such as doll's houses, toy farms and zoos, dinosaurs and play-people.

smooth pursuit *See* **tracking**.

socialisation The process by which children learn the culture or way of life of the society into which they have been born.

solitary play (solo play) Play in which a child plays alone, exploring and experimenting with objects.

spectator play Play in which children watch what others do, but do not join in.

spina bifida A condition in which one or more of the vertebrae in the backbone fail to form, as a result of which the spinal cord may be damaged. Spina bifida may be mild; in its severest form, however, it can cause widespread paralysis and a wide range of physical disabilities.

supine Lying on one's back, or face upwards. *Compare* **prone**.

symbolism Making one thing stand for another.

talipes A condition in which the foot is not in the correct alignment with the leg; it is sometimes called 'club foot'.

telegraphic speech (telegraphese) The abbreviation of a sentence such that only the crucial words are spoken, as in a telegram – for instance, 'Where daddy going?' or 'Shut door.'

temperament The style of behaviour that comes naturally, as for example a general tendency to be relaxed or excitable.

tracking (smooth pursuit) The smooth movements made by the eyes in following the track of a moving object.

transitional object *See* **comfort object.**

ventral suspension Supported in a prone position with a hand under the abdomen.

References and further reading

Bee, H. (1992). *The Developing Child* (New York: HarperCollins).

Bruce, T. (1996). *Helping Young Children to Play* (London: Hodder & Stoughton).

Bruce, T. and C. Meggitt (1999). *Child Care and Education* (London: Hodder & Stoughton).

Einon, D. (1985). *Creative Play* (London: Penguin Books).

Gopnik, A., A. Meltzoff and P. Kuhl (2000). *How Babies Think: the Science of Childhood* (London: Weidenfeld & Nicholson).

Karmiloff-Smith, A. (1994). *Baby It's You* (London: Ebury Press).

Lansdowne, R. and M. Walker (1996). *Your Child's Development from birth to adolescence* (London: Frances Lincoln).

Meggitt, C. (1999). *Caring for Babies: A Practical Guide* (London: Hodder & Stoughton).

Sheridan, M. D. (1997). *From Birth to Five* (London: Routledge).

Sheridan, M. D. (1999). *Play in Early Childhood* (London: Routledge).

Thomson, H. and C. Meggitt (1997). *Human Growth and Development.* (London: Hodder & Stoughton).

Useful addresses

Action for Sick Children (E)

Argyle House, 29–31 Euston Road, London NW1 2SD

Tel. 020 7833 2041 (09.00–17.00; recorded message out of hours)

Advisory Centre for Education (ACE)

Aberdeen Studios, 22–24 Highbury Grove, London N5 2EA

Advice line 020 7354 8321 (free)

Website www.ace-ed.org.uk

Association for Spina Bifida and Hydrocephalus (ASBAH)

England & Wales:

ASBAH House, 42 Park Road, Peterborough PE1 2UQ

Tel. 01733 555988

Website www.asbah.demon.co.uk/index.html

Child Growth Foundation

2 Mayfield Avenue, Chiswick, London W4 1PW

Tel. 020 8995 0257

Contact a Family

Contact a Family helps families who care for children with any disability or special need.

170 Tottenham Court Road, London W1P 0HA

Tel. 020 7383 3555

Website www.cafamily.org.uk/

Council for Disabled Children

Wakeley Street, London EC1V 7QE

Tel. 020 7843 6061

Cystic Fibrosis Trust

11 London Road, Bromley BR1 1BY

Tel. 020 8464 7211

Down's Syndrome Association

England & Wales:

155 Mitcham Road, Tooting, London SW17 9PG

Tel. 020 8682 4001

Website www.downs-syndrome.org.uk

Dyslexia Institute

133 Greshom Road, Staines, Middlesex TWl8 2AJ

Tel. 01784 463 851

Home-Start UK

The co-ordinating body for Home-Start schemes,which offer friendship,support and practical advice to families in difficulties with children under 5 in their homes.

2 Salisbury Road, Leicester LEl 7QR

Tel. 0116 233 9955

Invalid Children's Aid Nationwide (ICAN)

Barbican Citygate, 1–3 Dufferin Street, London EClY 8NA

Tel. 020 7374 4422

MENCAP (Royal Society for Mentally Handicapped Children and Adults)

Britain's leading charity working for and with people with learning disabilities, and their families.

England, Wales & Northern Ireland:

MENCAP National Centre, 123 Golden Lane, London EC1Y 0RT

Tel. 020 7454 0454

Website
www.harrogate.co.uk/mencap/mencap.htm

Muscular Dystrophy Group of Great Britain and Northern Ireland

7–11 Prescott Place, London SW4 6BS

Tel. 020 7720 8055

Website www.sonnet.co.uk/muscular-dystrophy

National Asthma Campaign

Providence House, Providence Place, London N1 0NT

Tel. 020 7226 2260

Helpline 0345 010203 (every day, 09.00–21.00)

Website www.asthma.org.uk

National Autistic Society

393 City Road, London EC1V 1NE

Tel. 020 7833 2299

Advice line 020 7903 3555 (Monday, Tuesday, Wednesday, Friday, 10.00–16.00; Thursday, 10.00–20.00)

Website carryon.oneworld.org/autism_uk/

National Children's Bureau

8 Wakley Street, London EC1V 7QE

Tel. 020 7843 6000

National Deaf Children's Society (NDCS)

15 Dufferin Street, London EC1Y 8PD

Tel. 020 7490 8656

Helpline 020 7250 0123 (Monday–Wednesday, Friday, 10.00–17.00; Tuesday, 10.00–19.00)

Northern Ireland:

Wilton House, 5 College Square, North Belfast BT1 6AR

Tel. 01232 313170 (voice and text)

National Eczema Society (NES)

163 Eversholt Street, London NW1 1BU

Tel. 020 7388 4097

Website www.eczema.org

Pre-School Learning Alliance (formerly Pre-School Playgroup Association)

69 Kings Cross Road, London WC1X 9LL

Tel. 020 7833 0991

REACH (The Association for Children with Hand or Arm Deficiency)

12 Wilson Way, Earls Barton, North Hampshire NN6 0NZ

Tel. 01604 811041 (answerphone)

Royal National Institute for the Blind (RNIB)

224 Great Portland Street, London W1N 6AA

Tel. 020 7388 1266

Website www.rnib.org.uk

Royal National Institute for the Deaf (RNID)

19–20 Featherstone Street, London EC1Y 8SL

Tel. 020 7296 8000

Tel. 020 7296 8001 (Minicom)

Website www.rnid.org.uk

SCOPE

The association for people with cerebral palsy.

12 Park Crescent, London W1N 4EQ

Tel. 020 7636 5020

Helpline 0800 626216 (England and Wales;
Monday–Saturday 11.00–21.00; Sunday
14.00–18.00)

Website www.scope.org.uk

SENSE (National Deaf–Blind and Rubella Association)

11–13 Clifton Terrace, Finsbury Park,
London N4 3SR

Tel. 020 7272 7774